JAN VERSCHUEREN'S DESCRIPTION OF YÉI-NAN CULTURE

VERHANDELINGEN

VAN HET KONINKLIJK INSTITUUT
VOOR TAAL-, LAND- EN VOLKENKUNDE

99

J. VAN BAAL

JAN VERSCHUEREN'S
DESCRIPTION OF YÉI-NAN CULTURE

EXTRACTED FROM THE POSTHUMOUS PAPERS

THE HAGUE - MARTINUS NIJHOFF 1982

ISBN 90.247.6185.9

Contents

Preface

Joannis Cornelis Verschueren (1905-1970) worked as a Roman Catholic
missionary in southern Irian from 1931 until his death on July 28,
1970. Following his ordination in 1930, his Congregation, the Sacred
Heart Mission, destined him for a function in the organization's
information and propaganda service in the Mother Country. For his
orientation, his superiors sent him on a visit to the diocese of
the Moluccas and South New Guinea, one of the Congregation's major
mission fields. Travelling through the Merauke area, he became so
fascinated by the missionary work being done there that he requested
and received permission to stay. After an introductory period at
Merauke, he was put in charge of the work in the middle and upper
Kumbe and Maro basins, a region which through his own activities
was soon afterwards extended to the Boadzi territory west of the
middle Fly. Initially stationed at Merauke, he later settled at
Bupul on the upper Maro. From here it was easier to serve the three
parts of his "parish" and pay an occasional visit to the upper Bian
area than from the Mission's main station at Merauke. As he was an
indefatigable walker, I suspect that this was not the only reason
for his retreat to Bupul. At Merauke he knew himself too much watched by his superiors. In the solitude of far-away Bupul he could be
himself and follow his inclinations to establish as many contacts
as he liked.

He did not return to Holland until 1946. Back in New Guinea, he
was stationed in the Mappi River region, whence he was recalled to
Merauke in 1953 to participate as an expert on local customs in the
researches of the team charged with the task of exploring the factors causing depopulation among the Marind-anim (the South Pacific
Commission Project S 18). He persuaded his fellow-members of the
team that the Yéi presented a good case for comparison with the
Marind. Having a different language and culture, they suffered from
a comparable population decline. The argument was valid, and in addition to other work on behalf of the project, he assembled and
sorted out his old fieldnotes on the Yéi, made a one-month trip
through the area, and proceeded to write the papers which are reca-
pitulated in the present volume. After a short visit to Holland
(1955) he was stationed in Wendu, on the coast, with the Kumbe
basin and the coastal area between Bian and Maro as his parish.
During his last years he lived at Merauke.

Verschueren was quite a character. He cared little about his personal appearance, and it took him some twenty years to get his Bra-
bant accent under control. Outwardly a countrified parish priest,
he was a keen intellect as well as an artist. The mural on the
vault behind and over the altar of his little church at Bupul was
of a bright beauty which deeply impressed me when in 1937 I paid

him a visit at his headquarters. He also had a gift for music, and
gave much of his time to the recording of native songs. Above all
he was interested in native culture, though not with the aim of pre-
serving it unchanged, for it was his calling to change it, spiri-
tually as well as materially, and he was always active in both
fields. One of his accomplishments in this respect was the estab-
lishment during the war of an agrarian school in the hinterland of
Merauke. He nevertheless was deeply convinced that the past is not
a thing to be thrown away. There is always something in a cultural
past to be proud of, something capable of merging with Christian
belief and liturgy. This was his ultimate object, which, combined
with a purely intellectual curiosity, induced him to probe as deeply as he could into his parishioners' cultural past. The results of
this research were published in a small number of articles which
contributed substantially to our knowledge of the original cultures
of the area. Really outstanding is his article on human sacrifice
in South New Guinea (*Indonesië* I, 1948), which was an eye-opener,
at least to me.

However, Verschueren had one handicap, namely his impetuosity. He
was always in a hurry, and more given to quoting from memory than
to the patient checking of details which were not to be found in
the fieldnotes at his immediate disposal. Yet there was one exception. When challenged to prove or disprove either one of his own or
of another person's assertions, he would go to the very heart of
the matter. Here he was at his best, which is the reason why his
major contribution to ethnography was provided by the letters written by him in comment of the original draft of my book *Dema*. They
cover hundreds of closely typed pages containing a wealth of hitherto unknown facts, which changed the old picture considerably. This
time these facts were well checked. I owe him a great debt for this,
though not for this alone, but also for that great friendship which
survived all differences of opinion. Actually, we disagreed often
and on various points. But the friendship which sprang up between
us during our common journey to the Boadzi in 1937 endured.

It is this debt which I must now try to repay. After Verschueren's
death, his *confrères* collected the papers from his legacy. They
were, as expected, in a state of chaos. His old friend, the late
Father P. Hoeboer, sorted them out and, moreover, typed out those
which might be of ethnographic interest, kindly putting a copy at
my disposal to see what could be done with them. I had to postpone
this scrutiny for many years, but when at last I was able to find
time to study them more closely, I discovered that they comprised
three categories: a collection of fieldnotes concerning the Boadzi,
four papers on the Yéi, and three Malay-language reports, written
in reply to questions put by Verschueren to Indonesian mission
teachers stationed in the Yéi-nan area.

The fieldnotes on the Boadzi have, for the greater part, been
summarized by Verschueren in his letters concerning *Dema*, in which
their contents have been published. In so far as these fieldnotes
contain additional information, this is too fragmentary to be of
any use, except to students with a wider knowledge of Boadzi culture than is available at present. They can be consulted in the
library of the Social Sciences Department of the Royal Tropical

Institute, in which also my correspondence with Verschueren is kept, together with his final comment on *Dema*, one year after its appearance. Here I have also deposited the papers being published in this book, together with the teachers' reports just mentioned. One of these is dated 1934, and I have good reason to suppose that the others are from the same period. Only some of the data presented in these reports were used by Verschueren and worked into his papers. Others were ignored by him for reasons which sometimes I am able to guess and sometimes do not know. Because I feel uncertain about the specific value of the writings of these teachers, I have made no more than a moderate use of them for my comments.

Before turning to Verschueren's papers themselves, a few words should be said about the only two ethnographic reports on the Yéi ever to be published, those by Wirz and by Nevermann. Both authors were professional anthropologists, the former of whom was well acquainted with the nearby Marind-anim, while the latter was a collector of ethnographic artifacts commissioned by the Berlin Museum to visit not only the whole of southern New Guinea, but also the New Hebrides and New Caledonia. Wirz's observations are limited but, on the whole, reliable and matter-of-fact and concisely formulated. Nevermann, on the other hand, was new to the area, had no other means of communicating with the natives (and the mission teachers!) than a rather limited Malay, and spent only two, at most three, weeks in the area. Yet he managed to fill well over 130 folio pages with an account of his experiences. Though his statements about what he himself observed are sometimes valuable, it takes quite some time to extract them from this verbose essay. I have seldom come across an anthropologist who could write so much about so little.

What Verschueren has to tell us is of a different nature altogether. It is genuine inside information. Though sometimes distorted by an over-emphasis on the differences between the Yéi and the Marind, which is aggravated by his conviction that the Yéi were sexually less depraved than their neighbours, his data as such are new and authentic. So authentic, in fact, that they repeatedly contradict his avowed opinion on the more "moral" character of Yéi-nan culture when compared with that of the Marind. Actually, he himself blocked the way to a more neutral interpretation of the facts presented by him by his insistence on including the Yéi in the depopulation research because they were culturally so different. In the context of the team's concern he was successful. With regard to the facts I can only say that they create a picture of a typical lowland culture with a surprising emphasis on headhunting, an uncommon way of segregating the sexes, and a highly elaborated system of phallic symbolism.

All this can be concluded from the four papers left by him, which, for the sake of convenience, I have labelled A, B, C, and D. Among these, ms. D stands apart. It comprises a four-page collection of myths which, unlike the three others, contains no reference to the author's participation in the Depopulation Research Project. Presumably, it is of a later date and was written as a contribution to some collection of native myths and folktales.

Manuscripts A, B and C all make mention of the Depopulation Re-

search Project as the reason for their writing. They are summary
descriptions of Yéi-nan culture of highly divergent lengths, comprising 18, 54, and 13 closely typed pages respectively. Only one
of them forms a complete whole by itself, namely ms. A. It is moreover the only one which bears a date: Merauke, 1954. Its final page
has a table of contents and a short glossary. Apparently it was
written as the author's contribution to the team's final report.
It was not included here in full, but was worked into a special
chapter better adapted to the immediate aims of the report than the
more comprehensive text of ms. A. The writer of the definitive text
of the report, Dr. S. Kooijman, is not to blame for this. He adopted this procedure reluctantly, expressing the hope that Verschueren's studies might one day be published in full in an ethnographi-
cal journal. Dr. Kooijman did more than this: he also attached Verschueren's ethnographic map of the area to the report, in spite of
the fact that it had no real bearing on the final text. Although it
is still mentioned there, the publishers, the Ministry of Overseas
Affairs at The Hague, did not attach it to the mimeographed text,
which, moreover, was distributed to only a very few institutions.
Those which I know received copies are, apart from the South Pacific
Commission in Noumea, the National Ethnographic Museum in Leiden and
the Royal Tropical Institute in Amsterdam.

Yet the map is of considerable importance in the context of Verschueren's combined papers, in particular mss B and C. I only realized this when, by a stroke of unusual luck, I came across it in my
private collection of maps which I was searching for something
else. The map indicates all the different *arow* (confederations of
clans) into which the Yéi are divided. It is published in the present volume after having the names and locations of the present-day
villages and the names of the rivers added, the latter as far as I
have been able to identify them from other sources. How the map
found its way to my library is a question which I cannot answer
with certainty. I probably owe its presence here to the kindness of
Dr. Kooijman, to whom I wish to express my sincere thanks for this
as well as for other reasons.

Manuscript A contains a very concise survey of Yéi-nan culture,
on which more detailed information is provided in mss B and C. Unfortunately, both are incomplete. B breaks off on p. 54, in the
middle of a myth, i.e. in the middle of the first section of the
chapter (obviously the last one of the essay) devoted to Religion
and Magic. The text of ms. C runs closely parallel to that of B,
but breaks off much earlier, somewhere in the middle of the chapter
dealing with the social organization of the Yéi.

The fact that the three documents overlap raises the question of
which is prior to which. The possibility of settling this question
on the basis of external evidence has disappeared with the originals
of the typescripts at our disposal. The only factual indication provided is the explicit reference in all three to the author's participation in the depopulation project as the immediate reason for
writing the paper concerned. This implies that they all originated
in the same period. A comparison of mss B and C - which are close
parallels - suggests that B is prior to C. B impresses me as having
been written more hurriedly than C. B contains superfluous details

and one or two poorly based value judgements which are lacking in
C. The question which remains is that of the relation between mss
B + C and A. A provides a good, convenient synopsis and presents
the data in the same order as B (and C). Being a good synopsis, it
will have demanded a good deal of prior spade-work. On these grounds
I presume that mss B and C were the author's first attempts at writing a survey of the main traits of the culture. He must have started
the work with that unbridled enthusiasm which was characteristic of
his way of doing things. While working on the chapter on Religion
and Magic, he must have realized that it was becoming altogether too
long and, besides, was in need of revision anyway. So he started a-
new. This then resulted in the more refined but only slightly more
condensed text of C. Realizing that this, too, was growing too long,
he again broke off, but now much earlier than before, and thereupon
wrote the concise text of A. The fact that the description of the
material culture and economy of the Yéi in ms. A is closer to the
text of C than of B supports this assumption. Though no definite
proof can be furnished, the assumption offers a satisfactory explanation for the fact that we are confronted here with three parallel
texts, which are often divergent in details, and of which only one,
the most concise one, was completed. A is the only document presenting a coherent survey of Yéi-nan ritual and magic.

The latter implies that precisely on the point of ritual and magic
the information is scant. No one deplored this more than Verschueren
himself. In 1967, while on long leave in Holland, he stayed for a
week or more with us, and on this occasion repeatedly expressed his
ardent wish to complete his Yéi-nan papers and prepare them for publication. This was in contrast with what he said about his fieldnotes on the Boadzi: these had been so badly damaged by mice and
termites that it would not be worth while bestowing much attention
on them. His papers on the Yéi, on the other hand, were still intact
and contained a great deal of new information - as, indeed, they do.
In any case their analysis has led me from one surprise to another
as gradually the picture unfolded of a typical New Guinea lowland
culture which is distinguished from its neighbours by its unique
mode of giving expression to the dialectics of sex and violence in
a male dominated society.

Two points remain to be discussed. In the first place that of the
manner of presentation of the three texts. Publication of the three
simply one after the other, leaving it to the reader to decide what
to do with them, would not be very helpful because the differences
between the texts raise questions which cannot be left unanswered.
Besides, this method of publication would be contrary to the intentions of the author, who had in mind a single comprehensive description. For this reason I considered it my duty to combine the texts
and to explain the choices I made wherever the differences between
the three texts created problems by means of annotations in square
brackets. Although this seemed reasonable enough, it soon got me
into difficulty with Verschueren's own interpretations of his data,
which constitute part of the text. I have already pointed out that
some of these are dubious, to say the least. Actually, the situation
is worse than that. Verschueren never for a moment realized the full

meaning and significance of the data which he presented. The materials collected by him are really surprising, but he never knew this. Should I, for formal reasons, let this go unnoticed and publish the text without pointing out what a really new kind of world the data open, whilst, by my familiarity with surrounding cultures, I am in a better position than practically anyone else to recognize their significance? I would have honoured his memory poorly if I had! Consequently, I have not withheld my comments. To avoid confusion between my own statements and Verschueren's texts, I have placed these sometimes in end notes (in contradistinction to the one footnote added by Verschueren), sometimes in square brackets within the text itself, but mostly as Editor's comments in separate indented paragraphs. The reader will find these paragraphs dispersed throughout the text and will find the notes and comments always sufficiently recognizable as my additions and as observations which are my personal responsibility. In this way an ethnographic description took shape which in some places differed in its order of presentation from that by Verschueren, but in every other respect always follows his text closely. I feel confident that this mode of presentation of his materials demonstrates more convincingly what a fine ethnographer he was than a method whereby I would have withheld my comments.

The second point to be raised concerns the linguistic position of the Yéi and the difficulties I had with the orthography of Yéi native terms. Our knowledge of the Yéi language is poor. On the point of vocabulary all we have to go by is a wordlist of 450 items arranged in non-alphabetical order as part of the comparative wordlist appended to Geurtjens' Marind-anim dictionary (referred to in the text as *Woordenboek*). Secondly there is Drabbe's grammatical outline of the Yéi language (10 pages), and Boelaars' comments on it in his dissertation (1950). The latter is important in that it informs us that linguistically the Yéi are related to the Kanumanim and the Trans-Fly people, and not to the Marind or the Boadzi. All this, however, offered no solace in my difficulties with Verschueren's often confusing spelling of Yéi-nan words. Consequently, I had to evolve my own system, which may be summarized as follows:
e designates in most cases the mute *ĕ* as in *novel*, but may actually also be pronounced as *é* (the *a* of *April*) or *è* (as in *bed* or French *père*), simply because the texts do not give any clarification on this point;
a may denote either the *a* of French *grand* or the *á* of German *Bahn*. Where there is evidence, occasionally, that it should be *á*, it is rendered as such;
j designates the sound often reproduced as *dj*, namely the *j* of *just*;
y is used where Dutch has *j*; it corresponds to the *y* of *yes*.
I had special difficulties with the *v* and *w*. In Drabbe's grammar the *v* is not mentioned, and only the *w* is. Verschueren uses the two consonants interchangeably. A case in point is the word *yevale* which is often spelt *yewale*. Apparently, the sound is somewhere in between the two; with the many dialectal differences in the Yéi language, this is very well possible. I solved the problem by opting for *yevale* because, in a dispute with Verschueren about a for-

mally related Marind term, he emphatically spelt the word out as
yĕvalĕ (cf. Van Baal 1966:243).

In conclusion, I wish to express my sincere gratitude to the Royal
Institute of Linguistics and Anthropology for its preparedness to
honour the memory of my late friend by publishing his intellectual
legacy in its Verhandelingen Series. I am indebted also to the
Institute's staff, in particular to Ms. M.J.L. van Yperen for her
highly appreciated revision of the English text, and to Ms. H.P.M.
Tigchelaar-Schulten for her effective secretarial and editorial
assistance.

Doorn, December 1982.　　　　　　　　　　　　J. van Baal.

Chapter I

Introduction

1. General introduction

In comparison with such neighbours as the Marind-anim and the
Boadzi, the Yéi-nan (*nan* = people, community) form but a small
tribe. They occupy the basin of the upper and middle Maro River
[and small parts of the eastern bank of the upper Kumbe River,
where formerly a few small groups of Yéi-nan lived in close proximity to the Marind]. The Maro River, called Burrau (= great river)
by the Yéi, is a swamp river, like most of the rivers in this part
of South Irian. They all derive their water from the numerous
swamps which overflow into the larger rivers through a huge net-
work of creeks and rivulets. The upper reaches of the big rivers,
such as the Maro, are flanked by extensive marshes which, during
the rainy West monsoon, are flooded by the abundance of water then
spilling over from the swamps. Seasonally the water level of the
rivers, in particular in the upper reaches, varies considerably.
For the Maro the difference between the East and the West monsoon
level comes to more than five metres. During the dry season the
rivers flow through vast, seemingly luxuriant meadows, the now dry
marshes. Once the rains have set in, these meadows change into wide
lakes, bordered by the often well forested more elevated grounds,
which in this part of the country are slightly hilly. Everywhere
in these temporary lakes, now teeming with waterfowl, small islands
overgrown with wild *jambu*[1] and eucalyptus testify that the terrain
is not as perfectly flat as it appeared during the dry season.
  In the northern part of the Yéi-nan territory higher grounds
which are never inundated are completely covered with rain forest
and eucalyptus trees. In the middle Maro region savannah areas
still occur, but in recent decades these have become progressively
overgrown with eucalyptus trees, which are multiplying with ever
increasing rapidity. At points where the higher ground borders on
marshes or rivers the natives build their settlements, preferably
on some elevated neck of land. Coconut trees indicate their location from afar.
  The occupants of this paradisiacal country, the Yéi, are slender-
er and leaner in build than the robust Marind. Yéi men, though
supple of movement, lack the dignity that is so typical of the self-
possessed Marind-anim. The latter never doubt their worth; they
speak of themselves as true humans, *anim-ha*. They can afford to be
frank and open in their dealings, whereas Yéi men impress us as
being rather shy and, at the same time, inclined to craftiness and
slight unreliability. Furthermore, the Yéi quickly copy the example
of foreigners. But where they accept the latter's rulings, one cannot be so sure whether this implies agreement.

Today, the Yéi-nan number less than a thousand people, the result
of a continuous depopulation process which did not stop until very
recently. Originally, i.e. before the occupation of southern Irian
by the Dutch (1902), there must have been well over 3,000, but imported diseases such as influenza and *granuloma venereum* have since
decimated them. A similar fate befell the much larger tribe of the
Marind-anim. But in spite of the fact that the campaign for the
eradication of *granuloma venereum*, started in the early twenties,
had been a success, the population decrease continued until the
early fifties. Only part of it was attributable to epidemic diseases, so that the suspicion then arose that the ultimate cause
had to be sought in the adverse effects of culture change. The
Netherlands New Guinea Government hereupon appealed to the South
Pacific Commission for financial and expert personnel assistance
for a project to explore the genuine causes of the depopulation,
primarily among the Marind-anim. The Commission agreed to help. A
research plan, officially known as Project S 18, was thereupon
drawn up. Its implementation was entrusted to a multidisciplinary
team, which I was invited to join as an expert on local customs
and culture.

Editor's comment. A few remarks must be made here, first of all
with regard to the impact of influenza and *granuloma venereum*.
Influenza first wrought havoc in 1918. Later epidemics were less
dramatic, but were all the same serious, notably that of 1937.
Yet influenza never had the deleterious effect on fertility as
venereal disease. Its occurrence in the Merauke district was
first reported in 1907, but it was not until 1921 that measures
were taken against it. These measures were drastic. Apart from
medication they included the suppression of feasts and rituals
among the Marind-anim, as well as the closing of their men's
and boys' houses. The Yéi-nan were compelled to give up their
custom of living in small settlements and came to be concentrated
in a number of larger villages, namely, from North to South,
Bupul, Samuting, Kwél, Jejeruk, Erambu, Torai (Komadeau), Kekayu
(Polka), Yawar, and Donggeab, 9 villages in all. (Surprisingly,
three of these villages are not mentioned by Verschueren in his
survey in Chapter II, Section 3, a point to which I shall return
in due course.) The campaign was successful in so far as after
1925 the birth rate increased considerably, though not sufficiently to offset the adverse effect of other diseases such as, primarily, influenza. Though soon after 1930 venereal disease stopped being a threat, the depopulation continued, and the suspicion
arose that the drastic intervention in their cultural life had
impaired the people's vitality (Van Baal 1940:397ff.).

    A second point to be made here is that Verschueren's estimate
of the original number of the Yéi is too high. It is based on the
assumption that originally the tribe comprised some 154 local
groups numbering on average 30 members. Consequently, he arrived
at a total number of 4,500 (in ms. B), which was such an improb-
ably high figure that he soon modified it to 3,000 in mss C and
A. The Depopulation Team's official Report did not copy his esti-
mate; it simply stated that it was impossible to make any esti-

mate at all. But this is also going too far. Considering all
things together, it seems to me that the original number of Yéi,
i.e. their number around 1900, may reasonably be assessed at a
little over 2,000, or maximally 2,400. This assumption is based
on the following data. The (incomplete) census of 1929 suggests
that at that time they numbered 1,640. By 1937 this had been
reduced to c. 1,150, in 1947 to 1,017, and in 1953 to 971 (*Rapport
Bevolkingsonderzoek Marind-Anim* 1958:204; Boldingh 1951/52:72).

One of the first decisions of the team was to include the Yéi-nan
in their researches. Differing markedly from the Marind-anim in
language and culture, and suffering a perfectly similar population
decrease, the Yéi-nan provided an excellent case for comparison. A
problem was that very little had been published on their culture
at the time. Dr. Paul Wirz, the well-known ethnographer of the
Marind-anim, had visited the Yéi-nan in the early twenties. The
results of his visit are recorded in Part III of *Die Marind-anim
von Holländisch-Süd-Neu-Guinea* (1925). However, his summary description of their social life covered little more than twelve pages.
Besides, it is open to the criticism that its author, pre-occupied
as he was with the Marind, tended to interpret his Yéi-nan data as
more closely resembling Marind-anim customs and institutions than
they actually did. Such misinterpretations were prompted by the
fact that the southern Yéi had, indeed, adopted a number of typical
Marind-anim practices. This was the result of a local acculturation
process which dated back to pre-colonial times and which was inten-
sified after the arrival of the Dutch. Thus the southern villages
(Erambu, Yawar, Polka and Donggeab) had adopted the Marind clan
names. The fact that they have not borrowed the Marind clan system
as such has given rise to a confusing situation which poses insol-
uble problems to outsiders trying to understand the marriage system.
Similar objections can be raised against the work of Dr. H. Nevermann, the second ethnographer to visit the Yéi. He travelled their
country in 1933 and published a rather superficial account of his
findings in the Baessler Archiv (1942).

   Editor's comment. Again a few points must be raised. In the first
   place, it should be noted that there is strong reason to doubt
   whether Verschueren ever read Nevermann's account himself. If he
   had, he might have been more moderate in his emphatic denial of
   the occurrence of totemism among the Yéi. It is true that Nevermann's visit was a short one, and also that his means of communication with the natives were inadequate, but he was no fool, and
   some of his data are of real interest to the student of Yéi-nan
   culture. On some points (i.a. on totemism) they provide supple-
   mentary information that should not be ignored.
      Verschueren held the view that the undeniable traces of totemism
   found among the Yéi were the result of their adoption of Marind-
   anim clan names. He strongly emphasized that the official registration of the Yéi by the local authorities between 1930 and 1932
   had accelerated this process. The registrars had to note down
   every individual's name and clan name, together with those of his
   wife and parents. They had started this work in the Marind-anim

region. When they came to the Yéi-nan, they asked them for such
clan names as had already become familiar to them. Poorly aware
that they were dealing with people of a wholly different culture,
they strongly encouraged the transposition of Yéi clan names into
Marind-anim categories. Among the southern Yéi, accustomed as
they already were to adapting their clan names to those of the
Marind, this posed no difficulties. For a fuller description of
this registration, see Van Baal 1966:71ff.

The present author had worked among the Yéi as a missionary from
1931 to 1947. During those years he had come to master their language reasonably well, which kind of proficiency time and again has
proved to be a principal prerequisite for understanding the basic
facts of a culture. His experiences of many years had been recorded
in a mass of fieldnotes, which were sorted out when, in 1953, his
association with the Depopulation Team offered him an opportunity
to concentrate on one specific aspect. He checked his material
during a one-month trip which took him through the whole of the
Yéi-nan territory, and then reworked it into his present contribution to the Team's report.
This general introduction would be incomplete without a few words
on the conditions of life in pre-colonial times. In that period the
Yéi-nan's relations with their neighbours were never friendly.
Though periods in which peace prevailed – a not uncommon thing
among mutually hostile tribes in New Guinea – did occur, lasting
peace was a real impossibility. It was precluded by the tradition
of headhunting, a form of warfare in which the Yéi-nan indulged
with as much zest as their neighbours. Notwithstanding, peaceful
contacts were not uncommon, as is borne out clearly by the adoption
of Marind-anim clan names by the southern Yéi and of the Yéi-nan
pöggul [ceremonial club] by the Marind.

Editor's comment. Here Verschueren is wrong. There is not a shred
of evidence that the Marind borrowed their *pahui* (the Marind
equivalent of the *pöggul*) from the Yéi (cf. Van Baal 1966:724-42).
Verschueren later conceded this. Another point which demands attention is that the Yéi were not at war with every Marind-anim
group. The southern Yéi maintained fairly permanent trade relations with the coastal Marind of Buti, who were eager buyers of
their canoes. Another export article of the Yéi was arrows. For
a more balanced account of warfare and trade between local Marind
and Yéi groups, see Van Baal 1966:700-6.

Relations between local Yéi groups among themselves were not always
peaceful, either. They were vaguely aware which groups formed part
of their own tribe and which did not, but there was little evidence
of tribal solidarity. Mutual assistance or the common celebration
of rituals between other than intermarrying groups were patently
absent. The one sign of tribal solidarity was the often heard as-
surance that the bodies of fellow-tribesmen who were killed in conflicts should not be beheaded or eaten. Such intratribal conflicts
were by no means rare. Even serious wars occurred. In fact, contacts between more distant Yéi groups, in particular between the

northern and southern groups, were rather exceptional. This is tes-
tified by the cultural differences between these two divisions of
the tribe. Among the southern Yéi there was a strong emphasis on
the cult of the *yevale* [translated by Verschueren as spirits,
supreme beings - the latter evidently a misnomer] and on magic[2],
whereas the northern Yéi, notably in Bupul and Kwél, were more
specifically concerned with the promotion of the social relations
ensuing from the dual division into Nak and Telle.

2. Material culture

The daily attire of the Yéi male consisted of little more than a
pubic shell or, in the case of older men, the sometimes slightly
ornamented husk of a dwarf-coconut, which served the same purpose.
On ceremonial occasions their dress was more elaborate. Really
ornate was their mourning-dress, which is described in Section 2
of Chapter VII. For festive occasions the men adorned themselves
with the feathers of the bird of paradise and of the xanthomelia
aurea and with a coiffure incorporating grass streamers of a somewhat simpler kind than the complex hair-lengthening pieces of the
Marind-anim. In later years, however, the Yéi, and more especially
the southern Yéi, increasingly often imitated the elaborate body
decorations of the Marind, in particular their ostentatious style
of hairdressing, little realizing that this elaborate pomp was
poorly suited to their slight stature, and provoked the ridicule
of their more robust neighbours. The latter had good reason for
mockery. For the ornamentation of the Marind reflected the orders
of their age-grade system. In the absence of such institutions
among the Yéi, their borrowed trappings did not reflect the bearer's
status but only his personal preferences, and impressed outsiders
as a ridiculous hotchpotch.

The Yéi women did not follow their consorts in such attempts at
imitation. They stuck to their traditional dress - the long, narrow
apron of bark fibres which is suspended at the front and the back
from the belt around the waist to just above the ground. On the
other hand, their mourning-dress was exceptionally elaborate (cf.
Chapter VII, Section 2).

In many respects the material culture of the Yéi must be said to
be poor. Their houses were spacious, open long-houses without walls.
These afforded shelter to the men and women of an entire settlement. One or more smaller sheds and huts served specific purposes.
They will be discussed in more detail in the next chapter, together
with the arrangement of the house and its division into a men's and
a women's quarter.

Plaiting was a female specialization. The wide mourning-hoods
and plaited cradles are among the finest products of their kind in
this part of New Guinea. The relevant techniques and the patterns
used were often imitated by members of neighbouring tribes, including the Marind.

Male tasks were the construction of canoes, the manufacture of
bows and arrows, and the carving of drums. Their tools were no more
than stone axes, boars' tusks, shells and fire. The canoes were
mostly small. They always had a pointed stem and were often ele-

gantly adorned. The oars were of the same type as those of the
Marind, and were often decorated with well executed carvings.

Editor's comment. Verschueren's comments on canoes are self-contra-
dictory. In one place he describes them as well finished, but in
several other places he expresses himself less flatteringly. He
further states that these canoes are mostly small. He argues that
the Yéi did not need big canoes because their raiding parties
never travelled by canoe but on foot. Towards that end the Yéi
laid out wide war-paths, which have remained visible up to the
present day. Nevertheless, in his description of the ceremonies
of the inauguration of a new canoe, the canoe in question is a
big one and evidently a war-canoe besides! For further details,
see Chapter VIII, Sections 1 and 4.

Bows were made of bamboo, like those of the Marind. Arrows were of
various kinds. The men devoted a great deal of time and attention
to their manufacture. The ornamental arrows made on the occasions
of mourning rituals and displayed at festive celebrations of all
kinds were the highly sophisticated products of good craftsmanship.
A long, wooden point was attached to a reed shaft and painted with
specific patterns in black and red, which were later varnished with
resin. Finally, the tip of the point was topped with a sharp cassowary nail, which was fastened by means of a mixture of resin, blood
and lime. Such arrows were rarely used for hunting; they were presented (and exchanged) as gifts on ceremonial occasions such as a
marriage, a mourning ritual, and so on.

Drums, like those of the Marind, were of the hour-glass type, but
were ornamented with patterns which are typical for the Yéi-nan.
The Yéi-nan were devoted carvers who knew their craft. This is also
evidenced by the realistic forms of the animal images carved on
house-posts and on the posts of bridges more recently constructed
by order of the government. [For additional information cf. Nevermann 1942:111, 200f.]

Musically, the Yéi-nan are more gifted than the Marind-anim, who
derive almost their entire repertoire from other tribes.[3] Their
ritual songs as well as their original dance melodies excel in melo-
dious quality and in mood-expressing power. Even the *gad-zi*, the
popular dance throughout the whole of the Merauke district, is sung
better here than anywhere else. Its melodies originated, in all
probability, in the Boadzi country. Rhythmically and melodically
they are more faithfully rendered by the Yéi than by most of the
other borrowing tribes.

3. Economic life

For their food the Yéi depend primarily on sago. Sago palms abound
in the marshes surrounding the rivulets which drain the swamps.
Fourteen different varieties of the palm used to be planted: some
with a smooth, others with a thorny bark; some high, some low; some
fast-, others slow-growing. There are some varieties which mature
in 9 years' time, whereas others need 15 years. Some produce good
midribs and/or leaves very suitable for thatching, while others

yield a white or yellow kind of flour, and others again a red flour.
For pounding the palm pith the Yéi women use the same techniques as
their Marind-anim sisters but, instead of wrapping the sago lumps
up in leaves, the Yéi women pour the flour into bags previously
plaited from rushes. Different, too, are their methods of process-
ing. They do not use hot stones for roasting or steaming the sago,
nor do they mix the flour with shredded coconut or coconut milk in
the same way as the Marind. They simply pack the dry flour into
bamboo leaves or into a section of the stem of a slender variety of
bamboo, and then roast it over an open fire or in hot embers. Coconut is not an important item of the daily menu. Though formerly
each settlement had its own coconut gardens, they preferably mixed
the sago flour with crushed young leaves and other greens.

The daily menu also included bananas, yams and taro. Whereas the
Marind laid out gardens only for festive occasions, for the Yéi
their garden produce was necessary to supplement the limited
yields of their sago groves. Besides, gardening was less laborious
for them than it was for the Marind, who, in their perfectly flat
natural environment, had to do all their planting in high garden-
beds which had to be raised from the loamy soil. The Yéi only needed to clear a relatively small part of the adjacent forest, which
patches they then cleaned thoroughly by pulling up the undergrowth
and burning the débris. After fencing in the clearing to protect
the garden against pigs, they planted their seedlings in the ash-
covered soil. These included banana-shoots, yam and taro cuttings,
sweet potatoes, sugar-cane, citronella-grass, and also fruit trees
of various kinds, primarily coconut but also breadfruit and *jambu*
[a *Eugenia* spec.].

Communal gardening was unknown among the Yéi, and they rarely
solicited the assistance of others for laying out a garden. Gardens
used to be made by a man and his wife, the husband doing the heavy
work and the wife the planting and weeding. [Evidently couples
wished to be left alone in their garden, practically the only place
where they could have sexual intercourse unobserved by others.]

Animal food was procured through hunting and fishing. The pigs
raised by the villagers were reserved for festive occasions. Hunting was a male pursuit. In the past, before the savannahs had
become overgrown with eucalyptus, wallabies were a favourite kind
of game. Today, hunting is confined mainly to the forest, where
tree-kangaroos, cassowaries, *cuscus* (opossums), birds and pigs may
be caught. Apparently the catch is rarely abundant: the Yéi consider
it worthwhile to hunt for mice in hollow trees, and for frogs in
the marshes. Collective hunts are rare. The fact that the term de-
noting such hunts, *ohan*, is a Marind term, suggests that collective
hunting has always been relatively rare. In practice, everyone preferably hunts for himself or, in the appropriate season, lays his
own private traps and snares.

Fishing is practised by both males and females. During the wet
season the catch is usually poor, but at the time the swamps are
drying up, barriers made of bamboo and sago-leaves are constructed
in the small rivers. These have one or more openings in which fish-
traps are placed; they yield a more satisfactory catch. [The texts
do not make any mention of angling or spearing fish, two techniques

usually reserved to the men. Yet it may be assumed that this practice is as common here as it is elsewhere. Fish-traps were usually
constructed by husbands and wives, the man as a rule making the
weir and the woman assisting him with this. That at least is what
some of the myths tell us, though our author suggests in one place
that the fences are made exclusively by the men.]

The women also used some fishing methods of their own. So they
would plait crude baskets (*bögguteo*) from sago-leaves, weight these
with heavy pieces of termite nests, and then let them down in the
water by the river bank. During the night shrimps and small fish
would enter these baskets, which were picked up again at dawn the
next morning. Another method involved the use of small round dip-
nets at the time the marshes were drying up. The women used these
to catch small fish and shrimps. Finally, mention should be made
of the use of poison to fish such small pools as never dry up during the dry season. [Whether this is a technique practised by males
or females is not mentioned.] In general, the yields from fishing,
like those from the hunt, were moderate. The size of the catch was
primarily dependent on the season.

Stimulants used by the Yéi are tobacco, betel and kava. Tobacco
was smoked in pipes (*báng*) consisting of a section of solid bamboo
with, near the end, a cross-piece of *bambu tali* [the Indonesian
term for a very slender variety of bamboo which is quite common in
these parts]. The cross-piece contains the tobacco, whereas the
main bamboo section is filled with a mixture of bark fibres and
shredded young sago-leaves to act as a filter. Tobacco (*képete* or
tsokkope) used to be cultivated in every garden. The seeds were
sown in places that were covered with a thick layer of ashes. Later
the seedlings were set out in soil which had previously been loosen-
ed. Though tobacco must have been known from early times, no mention
is made of it in Yéi-nan mythology.

Betel chewing is common, and is frequently indulged in by both
men and women. *Sirih* (a climbing plant which provides the leaves
in which the areca nuts are wrapped) and areca (betel) palms used
to be regularly planted.

Kava (called *wati* by the Marind) must have been introduced well
before colonial times. It is known here under various names, such
as *samai, bikwai* and *kidemi*. Like the Marind, they chew the stalks
and roots of the two years' old plant, spit the juice into a coconut bowl, and then drink this as an opiate before taking their
evening meal. Their methods of cultivating the shrub were as com-
plicated and laborious as those used by the Marind. However, the
Yéi were more moderate in their use of the drug. It was forbidden
to women and youngsters. In the past its daily use was restricted
to the older men. The younger men only drank it on festive occasions where many men were gathered.

Chapter II

Territorial, Clan and Moiety Organization

1. Editor's introduction

When sitting down to commit his knowledge of Yéi-nan culture to
writing, Verschueren intended to draw a picture of the *original*
culture (italics mine). Actually, this is the title he bestowed
on mss A and B. This implies that he did not try to describe the
cultural situation of 1947 or 1953, but that of the time prior
to the coming of the Dutch to the area; in other words, what he
gave was a reconstruction. This reconstruction is based on the
assumption that, originally, all the male members of every patrilineal clan (*jéi*) lived together with their wives and children
in one communal house, which constituted the clan settlement. The
latter was situated more or less at the heart of the clan territory, well away from the territories and settlements of other
clans. Adjacent clans each occupying a part of the same basin of
one of the numerous rivulets in the country constituted an *arow*
(litt.: area, river basin), which took its name from the river
concerned. Like the constituent clans, the *arow* was an exogamous
unit, all the clans of the unit belonging to the same exogamous
moiety. This ideal pattern is reflected in the list of *arow* and
jéi in Section 3 of this chapter and in the map accompanying it.
It is an almost perfect model of a highly segmented society,
divided into two patrilineal moieties, one of them counting 18,
the other 16 different *arow*, all of which were subdivided again
into a number of *jéi*, 154 for the two moieties combined.

Does this reconstruction of the "original" pattern really
reflect the social organization of eighty years ago? There are
two questions which arise in this connection, one a formal question, the other a substantive one. Let us deal first with the
formal question, viz. why should the term "clan" be used for the
jéi and not for the *arow*, the *jéi* to all intents and purposes
being nothing more than a subclan of the *arow*? This, indeed, is
what the model suggests. Nevertheless, Verschueren describes the
arow as a territorial group, whereas he always refers to the *jéi*
as the real genealogical unit; and it seems that this reflects
the usage of the Yéi themselves. There is no evidence for *jéi*
originating by fission from pre-existing *arow*. Moreover, the fact
that quite a number of the 154 *jéi* mentioned in the list are members of more than one *arow* contradicts the assumption that the
arow were the original clans. If the *jéi* had been the product of
fission of the *arow* of which it then formed part, it would still
belong to that *arow* and not to any other one. The explanation
of the surprising fact that the same *jéi* name is sometimes found
in different *arow* must be sought elsewhere, viz. in the frequent

instances of adoption necessitated by a strict system of marriage by sister exchange (see below, p. 16).

Of course this is not to deny the probability of frequent fission. The fission and fusion of clans are frequent phenomena in every segmented society. The smaller the constituent groups, the more frequent they will be, since they are the natural out-come of the caprices of demographic change. All I wish to point out here is that the genealogical units concerned were not *arow*, but *jéi*. *Arow* is, to all appearances, a geographic label used for a social unit which consists of a number of *jéi* cooperating, as we shall see, for the purposes of headhunting and canoe-building. It is not a genealogical designation. Though some of the *jéi* of an *arow* may have originated from one and the same founding *jéi* (as is only likely), we have not the slightest evidence that they all did so. Therefore I shall follow Verschueren's example and refer to the *jéi* as a clan. In this way we shall also remain closest to Yéi-nan usage. They sometimes also use the term *jéi* to designate a group of clans (cf. the names of the semi-moieties in Kwél as reproduced on p. 14 below).

The substantive question that must be raised is whether this representation of Yéi-nan society is consistent with Verschueren's opinion that the settlement is a clan settlement, uniting all the members of the clan in the one communal house, which is identical with the settlement as a whole. The answer is a decided no for two reasons, for the first of which I refer the reader to my discussion of Yéi-nan demography in Section 1 of Chapter I. There it has been argued that, if it is correct that a *jéi* numbered an average 30 members, this would put the total population at about twice the number the Yéi-nan can ever have comprised, namely 4,620 instead of something slightly over 2,000. Secondly, a settlement of only some 30 people (children included) is wholly inconsistent with the forms of social and cultural interaction described by Verschueren in his papers. These would be impossible in a settlement counting less than at least 70 people. What is worse, the average membership of a *jéi* was not 30 but – as anyone can figure out by dividing 2,400, the maximum total population, by 154 – 15 or 16, a number which practically excludes any form of cultural activity whatever.

That Verschueren's representation of the "original" settlement is untenable is fully corroborated by the report of the first government patrol which visited the area as early as 1908. It states that Komadeau (Torai) counted 15 open houses, accommo-dating about 200 people, whereas Bupul had, apart from three shelters, only one big house for some 100 people (*Verslag Mili-taire Exploratie* 1920:284 and 36). It is obvious, then, that a settlement can never have been purely a clan settlement, but must have been a place where several clans, all belonging to the same moiety, coresided, either all in the one house, or each clan (or one or two closely related clans) in a communal house of its own. Apparently Bupul represents the first type, Komadeau the second. We shall have to bear this in mind when turning pre-sently to Verschueren's description of the settlement, the more so because the facts confront us with the annoying uncertainty

of whether what Verschueren writes about the clan is valid exclusively for the *jéi*, or for the settlement as a whole, or (a problem raised by settlements counting more than one house) for a
house-community counting more than one *jéi*. Fortunately, the
problem is not unsolvable. The facts as set out in the following
sections (and also in later chapters) unanimously confirm the
view that the effective social unit is the group presided over
by a headman (*gab-elul*), which headman is invariably the leader
of a house-community, irrespective of the number of clans accommo-
dated in the house. This house-community is designated by the
name of one óf its constituent *jéi*. Because the Yéi use the term
jéi also to designate a group of closely assoċiated *jéi* (e.g. a
semi-moiety), the house-community can be described as a clan house
community without deviating from Yéi-nan usage. Obviously, the
use of the term *jéi* alternately in a wider and a narrow sense is
one of the main causes of the confusion which led Verschueren to
his untenable reconstruction of the original situation. With these
things in mind let us now turn to his description.

2. *The settlement*

The smallest territorial unit is the settlement, preferably located
on an extended spit of elevated land adjoining the marshes below.
Here a stretch of forest has been cleared to provide room for the
clan house and for the first gardens, where, after a number of
years, cŏconut palms will rise in many spots. Such a settlement is
always located close to the heart of the area of land owned by the
clan, in the vicinity of the sago groves bordering the creeks which
drain the forests and swamps. Yet the people do not reside here
permanently. During the dry season the paths to the settlement are
marked with taboo signs, and everyone departs for the creeks and
rivulets which now are abounding with fish and shrimps. There, in
the bush, they will find shelter under roof-shelters covered with
eucalyptus bark, a commodity which is always near at hand.
    The permanent settlement consists of one big house, a gable-
roofed open long-house without outside walls or substantial parti-
tions. The roof is supported by four rows of posts and covered with
eucalyptus bark. In the centre of the house stands a branched pole
which does not form part of the framework proper. It is adorned
with the war trophies of the local group: the skulls and the long
bones of its defeated enemies which hang on display here. The pole
marks the division of the house into a front half, the *soama*, and
a rear half, the *wake*. The *soama* is the exclusive domain of the
men, the *wake* of the women (and children). No one is allowed to
enter the half of the other sex. The rule is rigorously maintained,
except for children, who are allowed to go where they wish. Under
the roof everyone has his (her) own fireplace, the men in the
soama, the women in the *wake*. Here they spread their *wontje* (sleep-
ing-"mat"), usually the flattened spathe of the *nibung*-palm (*onco-
sperma spec.*) flower, or sometimes a discarded mourning-hood of
plaited bark fibre. A log is used as a head-rest. The various fireplaces are ranked. The older men and women have their fireplaces
near the centre of the house, the youngsters, according to sex,

at one of the ends. Tools, dancing paraphernalia and other private possessions are stored on the cross-beams or suspended from the forked poles which one finds throughout the house.

At the front and back of the house are open spaces, the front one (the larger of the two) reserved for the males, the rear one for the females. Special paths, one for each sex exclusively, give access to these open spaces, where during the daytime the members of the respective sex sit around and gossip or busy themselves with all kinds of chores. At the far end of the front yard, about 50 metres from the house, stands a simple shelter, the *korár bŏ*, which is the daytime residence of the adolescent males. Often a second shelter may stand nearby; it is the *korár ma*, the place where the adolescents may meet the mature men [if the *korár bŏ* is too small for this purpose].

The adolescent males are not allowed to be in the *soama* during the daytime. Early in the morning they are awakened by the headman (*gab-elul*), who takes them to the *korár bŏ*, under or in front of which they light a fire which must be kept burning all day to enable the men to warm themselves, to roast their food, and to straighten the arrows they are making. Although the rule that an adolescent male is not allowed to be in the communal house during the daytime is not as rigorously enforced as that which, among the Marind, prevents adolescents from entering the village by day, it is nevertheless maintained, and not without reason. The *korár bŏ* is usually erected at a place of strategic importance, which offers a commanding view of the entire surroundings. The *korár bŏ* used to function as a look-out post.

Finally, mention should be made of two other constructions, both relegated to a location in the bush in the immediate vicinity of the settlement. One is the open shelter constructed for a woman's forthcoming delivery, the other the hut for the ritual confinement of a girl who has just had her first menses.

The settlement[1] is the owner of the territory concerned, with its forests, swamps, creeks and plains and everything in or on them. Territorial boundaries are well defined; a swamp, a river or a creek, and on higher grounds a trail or anything else marks the border-line separating the territory of the group from that of its neighbours. There is no no-man's-land. The territory of the group is communal property, vigorously defended against any outsiders who may try to encroach upon it. Only members have a claim to the products or to certain parts of the territory as their personal property. If a member of the group comes across a tree which he thinks suitable for any future use such as the manufacture of a drum, an oar or a canoe, he need only mark this tree by a cut in its bark to make it his personal property, thus reserving it for future purposes. Similar rules are in force for hunting and fishing inside the territory's boundaries. By shooting a cassowary the animal becomes the hunter's personal property. Anyone who has assisted him in capturing the animal - e.g. by wounding it - has a right to a certain part of the catch. Analogous rules prevail with regard to gardens and sago groves. Every member of the local community has the right to lay out a garden or to plant sago in any spot inside the territory which has not been claimed by others. Everything thus

planted becomes his personal property, and his rights to the spot
continue for many years after the time when every trace of his
activities has vanished. No other member of the group will make a
garden or plant sago there.

Although the individidual's right of use to trees once planted
and to garden sites once cleared does not detract from the ultimate
right of the group to everything on or in its territory, the individual's right of use is not restricted to the person who has
created it: it is inheritable in the male line as the undivided
property of the planter's patrilineal offspring. It is a kind of
family right, shared communally by the originator's sons and grand-
sons [and, I presume, his daughters for as long as they remain in
the community house]. They do not divide the trees and garden sites
among themselves, but are allowed to make use of them whenever they
wish. Even so, a sago-tree on which a member of the family has bestowed special care, e.g. by adjusting its trunk, becomes that member's personal property.

Similarly, the fishing grounds (swamps and rivers) are intrinsi-
cally the property of the group as a whole. Nonetheless, by constructing a fishing barrier a man or a family (usually the construc-
tors are a husband and his wife) acquire a right which cannot be
ignored without the risk of a serious row, which, like every con-
flict over rights to land, calls for intervention by the *gab-elul*,
the headman of the territorial group.

Although in a headhunter society like that of the Yéi-nan the
headman is primarily a war-leader and the group's chief fighter,
he is also the custodian of the group's rights, and their defender
against outsiders whom he must prevent from entering the territory.
The headman sees to it that inside the group the members respect
its rules. He is an arbiter in intra-group conflicts and must
restore peace by enforcing the rules. As a *tuan tanah* [an Indonesian
term meaning "lord of the land", which the author may have taken
over from local Indonesian mission teachers but not from native
informants. It should not have been used here], the *gab-elul* is
also the settlement's ceremonial and ritual leader who fixes the
day and place of the group's celebrations, who arranges hunting and
fishing parties, and who plays a role in its religious activities.
His ritual function is reflected by the fact that he - and he alone
- may hold the *pöggul*, the ceremonial club. This object resembles
a staff which ends in a beautifully carved fretwork blade. Immediately below the blade a disc-shaped stone ring (*kupe*) has been
passed over the staff. During a war raid the *gab-elul* is supposed
to smash the fretwork blade on the victim first and then kill him
with a blow of the club (Chapter IV, Section 7). On ceremonial
occasions the *gab-elul* carries the *pöggul* as a sign of his office,
holding the weapon (suspended from a short sling across his shoulder) under his arm. When he wishes to sit, he puts the *pöggul* on
a low forked post next to his sleeping-place.

The settlement is the smallest territorial group. It is united
with several similar groups in a larger unit, the *arow*, usually
the basin of a rivulet, where the mutually cooperating settlements
have their territories, and from which this larger unit takes its
name. The constituting settlements and their headmen are all of

equal rank. The actual influence of a *gab-elul* is defined in practice by the size of his settlement on the one hand, and his personal talents on the other. However, if one of the constituent territorial groups is the host of the *arow yevale* - as is most often
the case - then the *gab-elul* of that settlement will *ipso facto* be
the leader of the *arow's* religious and magical ceremonies. Nevertheless, this superiority is, it seems, of a strictly socio-relig-
ious nature and has no territorial implications.

> *Editor's comment*. The *arow yevale* (*yevale* = spirit) plays a domi-
> nant part in the headhunting ritual. The *yevale* is expected to
> accompany the headhunters on their raids. It is obvious, then,
> that the *arow*, whatever else it may be besides, is the headhunt-
> ing unit.
>   The status and power of the headman as described by Verschueren
> impress me as being somewhat exaggerated. We have already noted
> that the designation of the *gab-elul* as *tuan tanah* must originate
> from some Indonesian mission teacher. These teachers were impor-
> tant informants to Verschueren. On his orders they wrote surveys
> of the customs and institutions in the respective Yéi-nan vil-
> lages where they were stationed. Some of these reports form part
> of Verschueren's literary legacy at present in my possession.
> They saw the *faits et gestes* of the Yéi through Indonesian eyes
> and interpreted them accordingly. As they originated from the
> Kai and Tanimbar Islands, *tuan tanah* was a familiar term to them.
> Also familiar was the notion that a headman has power and influ-
> ence, far more so than Papuan headmen naturally have. All this
> had its due influence on Verschueren, who, as a result of his
> education, presupposed the presence of authority in every human
> society and seized on every sign of it with an eagerness which
> sometimes got the better of his otherwise critical acumen.

3. The clan and moiety organization

The moiety dualism of the Yéi-nan has had a strong influence on
their marriage rules up to the present day. In 1953 moiety exogamy
was still consistently observed in the northern villages. In the
South, notably in Polka and Yawar, where Marind-anim influence has
always been strongest, observance of this rule has diminished. A
random survey showed that of all the marriages registered, some
25 % had been contracted in deviation from the rule of moiety exogamy.
   An intriguing form of double dualism has been noted in Kwél. Here
the *jéi* of the Nak were said to be either Méikiu or Benojéi, those
of the Telle either Dambujéi or Mogujéi. No information could be
obtained concerning the functions of this second bipartition. One
thing is obvious, however: it ignores the grouping of *jéi* into
arow. In one and the same *arow*, *jéi* which belong to either semi-
moiety are found. [But note the use of the term *jéi* in the names
of three of these semi-moieties! Apparently the term is also appli-
cable to larger units than a clan.]
   In the list of *arow* and *jéi* now following, the *jéi* are listed in
the column of the moiety of which they form part, where they are

arranged in the order of the *arow* [and of the present-day village]
to which they belong. This arrangement clearly demonstrates the
interconnections between the territorial and genealogical organization of the Yéi.

Editor's comment. On one point the list is regrettably incomplete.
For three of the southern villages have been omitted, namely
Jejeruk, Torai and Donggeab. However, on comparison of the list
of *arow* with the map, we discover that these *arow* and *jéi* of
these three villages must have been included under the name of
another village.

For convenience of analysis the repetition of the same name
under different headings has been indicated by a reference accordingly between brackets at each recurrence of such a name in
the list. Other information, too, has been added in the same way,
e.g. where the reading of the list in ms. C differs from that of
the one being followed here.

Finally, to mark the beginning of a new series of *jéi* grouped
together in a single common *arow*, I have added the word *jéi* to
the name of the first *jéi* of the new series.

Of the 33 *arow* names found on the map, five have not been
mentioned in the list, namely Ié, Tau, Marma, Tsöluk, and
Beyelter. That Beyelter is also the name of a *jéi* of the *arow*
Berapto (Erambu) does not help us in any way. Berapto is indicated on the map, and consequently the case of Beyelter hardly
contributes to the solution of the problem created by the fact
that the five *arow* omitted from the list are offset by six out
of the 34 *arow* of the list not occurring on the map, namely
Pírpa, Aroar, Kassebák, Teli, Tawani and Kolpa. It seems a fair
assumption that some of the names missing from either will be
identical, but the supposition that neither the list nor the map
is entirely complete is equally fair.

A more intriguing point is that of the *arow* assigned to more
than one village. A striking case is that of Tanas, which shares
all its *arow* with Bupul, sometimes with exactly the same *jéi*, but
often with *jéi* which either are exclusive to Tanas or belong to
a different *arow* of Bupul from that of Tanas. The same phenomenon
recurs with Yawar and Kwél, which share the *arow* Imbias with all
its constituent *jéi*. This is not the case with the *arow* Obat Nak
which Yawar has in common with Polka; the *jéi* of Yawar are different ones from those of Polka. In all these cases a single
explanation obviously suggests itself: Tanas (better known to
old-timers as Samuting) and Yawar are Protestant villages; Bupul,
Kwél, Erambu and Polka are Roman Catholic. Apparently, the division between Catholics and Protestants has split up the *arow*,
and often even the *jéi*.

This is quite a satisfactory explanation to those who tend to
look at things from the mission point of view; but more sophisticated anthropologists might object that the choice of a different denomination might equally well be the result of pre-
existing controversies between the relevant groups. They have a
convincing case in that of the *arow* Seláb which Bupul shares with
Kwél, with only one *jéi* differing. Bupul and Kwél are both Cath-

olic; consequently, difference of denomination cannot play a role here. Of course one might claim that the inclusion of Seláb under both Bupul and Kwél is due to an error committed by Verschueren, a man inclined to work in a hurry. I would not like to contradict this, but the fact that he would have committed this error twice, in ms. B as well as in ms. C, while in both cases he went to the trouble of laboriously noting down all the names of the relevant *jéi*, is more than can, in all fairness, be attributed to my late friend's hurry. In my opinion it all reflects the basic characteristic of a segmented society composed of small units. Such a society is always oscillating between fusion and fission, always hovering between one combination or the other. Verschueren has tried to give a static picture of the organization of this society - a vain effort. And here obviously lies the key to the problem of why he gave up every attempt at specificity when coming to the description of the social organization of the southern villages. In this area the practice of moiety exogamy is breaking down (see above) - a violation of the ideal pattern which made it even more difficult to trace its prevalence in the distribution of *arow* and *jéi* over the various villages of the area. This attempt with regard to the northern area, which, being closest to the mission station, he knew best of all, must have taken up so much of his energy that, when he came to the description of the southern area, he renounced every effort at investigating how the members of its *arow* and *jéi* were distributed over the villages in which the old-time clan settlements had congregated.[2]

The table has the important merit that it demonstrates clearly that the *jéi* are by no means as strictly localized as Verschueren supposed. Various factors contributed to this. We have already mentioned the inevitability of fusion and fission as a result of unequal demographic growth. Another factor is the system of marriage by sister-exchange. The Yéi were strict on this point. The rule forced parents of an unequal number of sons and daughters to adopt an exchange sister for a son or an exchange brother for a daughter every time another family of the always small clan house community was unable to make one available. Young adolescents must have been frequently adopted as exchange brothers in families of a different settlement and *arow* from their own, provided it was one of their own moiety. In settlements counting about 70 people each, problems of this kind must have been the order of the day. It is not improbable that these adopted young men retained their clan name and thus, after their marriage, founded a new branch of their original *jéi* in the settlement where they had been adopted. This would account for the curious distribution of some of the *jéi* over quite a variety of *arow*.

In this context another fact is of interest. There are many cases of *jéi* being represented in different *arow*, but not a single one in an *arow* of the opposite moiety, a circumstance which strongly confirms the significance of the moiety dualism.[3]

VILLAGES, AROW, JÉI AND MOIETIES

Village	Arow	Jéi	
		Nak	*Telle*
Bupul	Boad (cf. Tanas)	Bino *jéi* (cf. Kwél: Béo) Tjobu Kabel (cf. Kwél: Palda) Böl (cf. Kwél: Danebob) Tsáwer (cf. Buwím) Kewamme (cf. Tanas)	
	Jöju		Kojaro *jéi* Mago (cf. Bomön; Tanas: Udöp) Anggro (C: Anggo) Kamme (cf. Bomön, Yánd; Tanas: Yánd & Udöp) Wége Per (cf. Udöp; Tanas: Bomön)
	Buwím	Mekiu *jéi* Marpe (cf, Kwél: Sowai) Alo Tsáwer (cf. Boad) Nanggobe Wan (C only)	
	Seláb (cf. Kwél)		Dago *jéi* (cf. Kwél; Tanas: Udöp) Gamme (cf. Yawar: Teli) Dambu (not in C; cf. Kwél; Tanas: Udöp) Wálke (cf. Udöp & Kwél) Bakke (cf. Kwél: Seláb & Tsaru) Inage (cf. Kwél)

VILLAGES, AROW, JÊI AND MOIETIES (Cont.)

Village	Arow	Jêi		Telle
		Nak		
Bupul	Udŏp (cf. Tanas)			Iriánter jéi (cf. Kwél: Kege)
				Wálke (cf. Seláb; Kwél: Seláb)
				Per (cf. Jŏju; Tanas: Bomŏn)
				Gwammer (cf. Kwél: Makkedi; Polka: Omboge)
	Bomŏn (cf. Tanas)			Mago jéi (cf. Jŏju; Tanas: Udŏp)
				Wŏnni (cf. Tanas: Yánd)
				Kamme (cf. Jŏju, Yánd, Tanas: Yánd & Udŏp)
	Ieb (cf. Tanas)	Kárko jéi (cf. Tanas; Kwél: Palda)		
		Kŏnni (cf. Tanas)		
		Sikow		
		Kewan (cf. Tanas; Polka: Sembe)		
	Yánd (cf. Tanas)			Mogu jéi
				Kamme (cf. Jŏju, Bomŏn; Tanas: Yánd & Udŏp)
				Kwammeter (cf. Tanas: Bomŏn)
				Láuw
				Okéter
				Gebo (cf. Tanas)
Tagebou		Mandal jéi		

VILLAGES, AROW, JÉI AND MOIETIES (Cont.)

Village	Arow	Jéi	Telle
Tanas (Samuting)	Boad (cf. Bupul)	Kellu jéi (cf. Kwél: Omod)	Dambu jéi (cf. Bupul & Tanas: Selāb)
	Udōp (cf. Bupul)	Kwamme (cf. Bupul: Boad)	Mago (cf. Bupul: Jōju & Bomōn)
			Kamme (cf. Yánd; Bupul: Jōju, Bomōn & Yánd)
	Bomōn (cf. Bupul)		Dago (cf. Yánd; Bupul & Kwél: Selāb)
			Kei jéi
	Ieb (cf. Bupul)	Kárko jéi (cf. Bupul; Kwél: Palda)	Per (cf. Bupul: Jōju & Udōp)
		Kewan (cf. Bupul; Polka: Sembe)	Kwammeter (cf. Bupul: Yánd)
		Kōnni (cf. Bupul)	
	Yánd (cf. Bupul)		Wōnni jéi (cf. Bupul: Bomōn)
			Dago (cf. Udōp; Bupul & Kwél: Selāb)
			Kamme (cf. Udōp; Bupul: Jōju, Bomōn & Yánd)
Kwél	Selāb (cf. Bupul)		Gebo (cf. Bupul)
			Bakke jéi (cf. Tsarup & Bupul)
			Dago (cf. Bupul; Tanas: Udōp & Yánd)
			Dambu (cf. Bupul; Tanas: Udōp)
			Youter
			Wálke (cf. Bupul: Selāb & Udōp)
			Inage (cf. Bupul)
	Beo	Bino jéi (cf. Bupul: Boad)	
		Jabuter	
		Keipe	

VILLAGES, AROW, JÉI AND MOIETIES (Cont.)

Village	Arow	Jéi	
		Nak	*Telle*
Kwél	Omod	Menakon jéi Kellu (cf. Tanas: Boad) Tamol Belo (cf. Danebob; Polka: Obat Nak & Sembe) Mér Unke (cf. Palda)	
	Kege		Bai jéi
	Tsarup		Kondeter Iriánter (cf. Bupul: Udöp) Bakke jéi (cf. Seláb (also Bupul)) Wán Kwalme
	Danebob	Mékio jéi Belo (cf. Omod; Polka: Obat Nak & Sembe) Tjölbuter Böl (cf. Bupul: Boad)	
	Palda	Unke jéi (cf. Omod) Kárko (cf. Bupul & Tanas: Ieb) Járkarow Kabel (cf. Bupul: Boad)	
	Makkedí		Gwammer jéi (cf. Bupul: Udöp; Polka: Omboge) Wonin Kwéál (cf. Yawar: Teli) Galo Nambuter Kwod

VILLAGES, AROW, JÉI AND MOIETIES (Cont.)

Village	Arow	Jéi	
		Nak	Telle
Kwél	Kéikei	Kepal jéi	
		Keke	
		Gubá	
	Sowai	Marpe jéi (cf. Bupul: Buwím)	
		Paketjowter	
	Imbias (cf. Yawar)	Mako jéi (cf. Yawar; Polka: Tawawi)	
		Takuter (cf. Yawar)	
		Ngeiwal (cf. Yawar; Polka: Obat?)	
Erambu	Bárki	Jeraketraw jéi (C: Jeraketjow)	
		Mo	
		Kwosu	
	Kwitale		Bo jéi
			Görgwa
			Barpe
			Mur
	Pírpa	Göbbe jéi	
		Nekel	
	Aroar		Mowliter jéi
			Tsogel
			Koluter (C: Kolu)
			Kabo
	Kassobák		Yebutjater jéi (C: Yebutjetjer)
			Waliter

VILLAGES, AROW, JÉI AND MOIETIES (Cont.)

Village	Arow	Jéi	
		Nak	*Telle*
Erambu	Berapto	Awaliter *jéi* Upage Beiwarter Beyêlter	
Yawar	Imbias (cf. Kwél)	Mako *jéi* (cf. Kwél; Polka: Tawawi) Takuter (cf. Kwél) Ngeiwal (cf. Kwél)	
	Teli		Kapeiter *jéi* Gamme (cf. Bupul: Seláb) Kamme (cf. Bupul: Jóju, Bomõn & Yánd; Tanas: Udõp & Yánd) Gamuter Tsoggel Irterna Kwéál (cf. Kwél: Makkedí) Belmao *jéi* Telle Mánke Jeroke Peyénke
	Obat (Telle)		
	Obat (Nak)	Tsammer *jéi* Kupele Tsarreke	

VILLAGES, AROW, JÉI AND MOIETIES (Cont.)

Village	Arow	Jéi	
		Nak	*Telle*
Polka (Kekayu)	Obat (Nak)	Ngiwal *jéi* (cf. Kwél & Yawar: Imbias; note spelling diff.) Wonán (cf. Sembe) Kwirku Belo (cf. Sembe; Kwél: Omod & Danebob) Ipi	
	Omboge		Dago *jéi* (cf. Kwél & Bupul: Seláb; Tanas: Udŏp & Yánd) Gwammer (cf. Bupul: Udŏp; Kwél: Makkedí) Yowa Dagel
	Yób		Gal *jéi* Kopalo
	Sembe	Wonán *jéi* (cf. Obat Nak) Kewan (cf. Bupul & Tanas: Ieb) Tabel Owan (C: Owam) Belo (cf. Obat Nak; Kwél: Omod & Danebob)	
	Tawawi	Mako *jéi* (cf. Yawar & Kwél: Imbias)	
	Wanon		Tar *jéi* Wŏbbetu Bonge Gwale (cf. Kolpa)
	Kolpa		Gago *jéi* Gwale (cf. Wanon) Yoakel

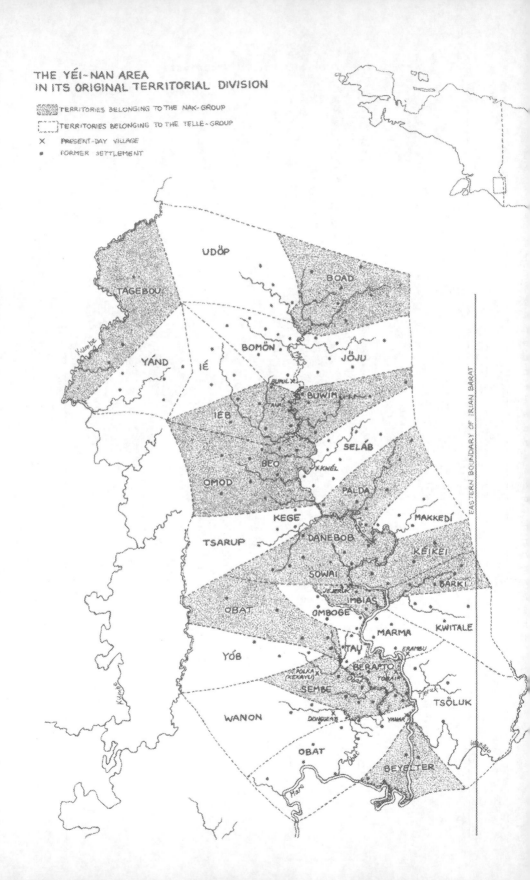

THE YÉI-NAN AREA
IN ITS ORIGINAL TERRITORIAL DIVISION

TERRITORIES BELONGING TO THE NAK-GROUP
TERRITORIES BELONGING TO THE TELLE-GROUP
X   PRESENT-DAY VILLAGE
*   FORMER SETTLEMENT

UDÖP

BOAD

TAGEBOU

YÁND

BOMÖN

JÖJU

IÉ

IEB

BUWIM

SELÁB

BEO

KNEL

OMOD

PALDA

MAKKEDÍ

KEGE

TSARUP

DANEBOB

KÉIKEI

SOWAI

BARKI

OBAT

IMBIAS

OMBOGE

KWITALE

MARMA

YÓB

TAV

ERAMBU

BERAPTO

AOLKA
(KEKAYU)

TOBAIR

SEMBE

TSÖLUK

WANON

DONGKEB

YINMA

OBAT

BEYELTER

EASTERN BOUNDARY OF IRIAN BARAT

Chapter III

Kinship, Marriage, and Conjugal Life

1. Kinship

The kinship system of the Yéi-nan is patrilineal. Marriage is viri-
local and dominated by the rules of sister exchange and moiety
exogamy. Marriage by payment of a brideprice was unknown.

Kinship terms are as follows:

yeboi	fa, fabr
man	mo, mosi
natau	fasi
eiy	mobr
nagei	br, fabrso
nagár	si, fasida
eiye por	mobrso
bei	fasiso, mosiso, fabrda
elul por	so
menötjer por	da
néam	grandfather, grandmother, grandchild; wifa, wimo, wifasi, wifabr, wimosi, wimobr; hufa, humo, hufasi, humosi, humobr, hufabr
néam-néam	great-grandparents
morei (plur. morro-morro)	(great)-grandparents, (great)-grand-children
modar-por	wibr
nakom	wisi
nower	hubr
magér	husi
nát	exchange sister

Alternative terms for father and mother are *auw* and *nai* respectively.
Tsampor, ursár, and *mandalbai* added to the terms *nagei* (br) and
nagár (si) designate the eldest, the middle and the youngest of
three brothers or sisters.

Editor's comment. The list of kinship terms is defective and in-
accurate. The terms for son's wife and daughter's husband, for
mobrda and for exchange brother are lacking. That the term for
grandparents and grandchildren is reciprocal I had to find out
from the comparative wordlist in Geurtjons' *Woordonboek* of the
Marind language (pp. 406-7). No mention has been made of terms
of address and their use. Presumably *auw* (fa) and *nai* (mo) are
such terms, but I have no certainty on this point. Really unfor-
tunate is the absence of information on the classificatory use
of kinship terms. There is one exception to this: the term *néam*.
Its use vis-à-vis parents-in-law might have been instructive if
we had known the terms used for son- and daughter-in-law, which,

as was noted above, have been omitted. We also look in vain for
information on the effects of exchange marriage on the kinship
terms used by the children of such marriages for their mother's
exchange brother and father's exchange sister. Are they really
the same as those used for a mobr or fasi who is not at the same
time fasihu or mobrwi?

How little the author has really gone into the ins and outs of
the kinship system is demonstrated by his repeated assertion
(though not included in the present edition of his papers) that
among the Yéi the mother's brother has no specific functions at
all, a statement which is definitely contradicted by his own
data on initiation and canoe feasts. Actually, the assertion is
simply another of the exaggerations to which he fell prone whenever he wished to contrast the customs of the Yéi with those of
the Marind. Among the latter a mother's brother normally lives
in the same village as his sister's children, where he acts as
their mentor and as the boy's pederast. His functions are far
more comprehensive than among the Yéi, but this does not mean
that he exercised no functions at all with regard to his sister's
children among the latter. As he lives in a different, more or
less distant settlement here, the performance of such functions
is necessarily restricted to special occasions.

2. Marriage

Marriage is patrilocal, and must be contracted by sister exchange
with a young man of an *arow* (and settlement) of the opposite moiety.
Consequently, the bride always comes from quite far away. The rules
of the marriage trade are exacting, and often the parents concerned
will take the necessary steps when the prospective spouses still
are children, even small children.

The ideal situation is that a boy has a sister of his own who can
be given away in exchange. If he has no real sister an adoptive
sister may do. If there is neither, a young man (or his parents)
must try to find a girl of his own settlement whose parents are
willing to give her to him as his exchange sister. [Verschueren
says here that she must be of the same *jéi*, but his comment that
"people of another settlement, even if they are of the same *arow*,
are not sufficiently interested in the marriage of a boy of another, related *jéi*" makes it clear that he had in mind settlement.]
Other means for contracting a regular marriage were practically
non-existent. A girl from another but related *jéi* [settlement!]
could only be acquired as an exchange partner in the exceptional
case that this other *jéi* still had to pay compensation for a murder
committed in previous years. This happened once in Bupul, where
Lucia Wale of the Inage-*jéi* was handed over as an exchange sister
to the Kojaro-*jéi* because long ago, in Powoïter, a man of the
Kojaro had been murdered by an Inage man.

It was not possible among the Yéi to obtain a marriage partner
by promising that a daughter born of the marriage would, in time,
be ceded to the bride-givers to compensate for their present loss,
a solution not uncommon among the Marind. For a sisterless young
man the only way out was that of elopement with a widow who had

not been taken in second marriage by her late husband's brother. On such occasions the pair usually enjoyed the secret aid of other women.[1] Elopement with a girl hardly ever occurred. It constituted a *casus belli* which necessarily resulted in at least one murder in revenge.

Consequently, parents of an unequal number of sons and daughters normally tried to achieve a balance either by adopting a boy or a girl as a prospective exchange partner for a daughter or son, or by giving a supernumerary son or daughter to a couple in search of one. This was not always easy because the Yéi are fond of children and like to have a large family. Childless couples invariably try to acquire children by adoption. They may even ask for one, though (except between brothers) it is bad form to do so. In case of childlessness it is more proper to wait until some other couple takes pity. [Of course, this is quite a different case from that of the adoption of a child as an exchange brother or sister. From what has been said on this point, it must be concluded that active attempts at acquiring a child for this reason can only have been considered improper if the request were addressed to parents who were relative strangers.] Friendship, too, can be a reason for giving a child away, even if the friends belong to different settlements. However, a child can never be given to a family of the other moiety, because this would result in a boy marrying his own sister. [Note that here the term sister is used in a wide, classificatory sense!]

A more violent means of acquiring a child is by capturing one on a war raid. Such a child is adopted into the warrior's own *jéi*. In more recent years a new method of acquiring children has evolved, namely that of buying them from foreign tribes for imported goods which are so valuable to these tribes that they are willing to sacrifice a child for them. The custom has sprung up since the arrival of the whites. For the Yéi the only suitable partner in this trade is the Boadzi.

Editor's comment. Verschueren makes no comment about what happened upon the adoption of a boy as an exchange partner. Obviously, he stayed in the settlement of his adoptive parents after his marriage.

Marriage is, in principle, monogamous. The celebration of a marriage ceremony is restricted to a man's first marriage and, though polygyny occurs, only the first wife is considered to be her husband's proper wife.[2] For polygyny various arguments are put forward, viz., in order of their social importance:
1. Sterility of the wife. As children are the real aim of a marriage, sterility is a normal, and also the most frequent, reason for taking a second wife.
2. Headmanship. People say that often it is not so much a case of the headman himself desiring a second partner, as of eagerness on the part of many women to share in the power and influence which go with headmanship and a polygynous marriage generally.
3. Levirate. A widow used to be inherited by her late husband's brother. Yet, he might refrain from taking her in marriage if he was too much in love with his own wife, or - as was more fre-

quently the case - if the latter too "effectively" resisted an
extension of their household.
4. A polygynous family is more productive, has more gardens, better
food and, consequently, more prestige.
5. The taboos on sexual intercourse preceding and following his
wife's delivery might sometimes persuade a husband that, sexually, one wife did not suffice.

The procedure followed in concluding a second marriage is simple.
[Verschueren here ignores the circumstance that the man has to cede
a "sister" anyhow.] The woman prepares sago for her prospective
husband, which, at her request, her brother hands over to him, saying: "My sister sends you this sago". If the man accepts the sago,
the woman immediately collects her belongings and follows her new
husband to his house. Even if the second wife is a young, unmarried
girl, this is all that takes place in the way of ceremony.

A first marriage must be celebrated by the two contracting parties;
it is a simple celebration, admittedly, but all the same an official ceremony. Once agreement has been reached by the parents of
the prospective spouses, the two fathers with their brothers and
such local prominent people as happen to be present sit down together in the bride's father's settlement to drink kava, the kava
being presented by the boy's father. It is a trivial ceremony,
serving no other purpose than to confirm that the bride has been
promised. If the girl is adolescent, her prospective mother-in-law
will fasten a thin string round her wrist as a public sign that
the girl is betrothed.

The marriage feast is celebrated in the settlement of the boy.
The exact date of the ceremony has been announced by a *tui*, a section of a dry sago-leaf rib into which as many little sticks have
been thrust as there are nights left to sleep. In the meantime the
boy's family sets out to pound sago and to collect game, fish, garden produce, kava, betel, and so on. On the appointed day, the
bride is escorted to the boy's settlement. They do not enter it.
The men sit down in a group beside the trail, at a distance of some
50 metres from the settlement. The women and the bride sit a little
farther off.

In the settlement the women have cleaned the *wake* (the women's
part of the house) and strewn the ground with croton twigs, flowers
and fragrant leaves. They now strew the path leading from the *wake*
to the place where the men are awaiting their guests. Then the
young men, the bridegroom's age-mates, leave the *soama* (the men's
part) with the bridegroom, and escort him to the spot where the
kinsmen of the bride are waiting. The moment of their arrival is
the moment for putting the finishing touches to the bridegroom's
apparel, as well as to that of the bride. The latter is done by the
women who have brought her and who now escort her to the spot where
her kinsmen and her bridegroom are waiting. On her arrival the
bridegroom arises. A friend hands him a bow and an arrow. The bow
is carried, as usual, with the bowstring turned up. The girl seizes
the rear end of the bow, and then everyone, the groom in front with
the bride closely behind him, departs for the decorated *wake* of the
bridegroom's kin.

Here the women of the house sit in a wide semi-circle, with the
bridegroom's mother in front. When the groom has arrived in front
of her, he bends his knees, turns around, and returns to his
friends, who are waiting in front of the *wake* and now accompany
him to the *soama*. In the meantime the bride has seated herself on
the lap of, first of all, her mother-in-law, and then, one by one,
the laps of all the other women sitting in attendance. Then the
women arise, and they all give the bride a new *sinak* (apron) which
she puts on the one over the other.

That night the men and women stay each in their own part of the
house. In the *soama* coconut bowls are placed in a row, and the
youngsters are invited to fill them with kava for the guests (cf.
Chapter I, Section 3). Every time a guest has emptied his bowl he
beats the open end on the ground in front of his hosts, "to let
the kava catch". Now food is brought from the *wake*. The father
(and in the *wake* the mother) of the bridegroom are the last to be
served. The night is passed quietly. There is no dancing. [There
cannot be any, either, as the kava, always consumed undiluted, does
not act as a stimulant but as an opiate.]

The next morning the bride's family says goodbye and departs for
home. The young women of the settlement, however, assemble and set
out for the sago-grounds with the newly wed woman in their midst
to make a new plantation. This ceremony is called *negöl wagedo
topo*, "the playful cleaning of a garden". It is, indeed, quite an
occasion and is celebrated with great hilarity. Not one man, not
even the new husband, follows the women, who return only toward
nightfall.

Editor's comment. One of the teachers' papers reports that in
Donggeab the women's celebration in the sago grove was followed
by other festivities, including an official meeting between the
bride and bridegroom and a visit to the settlement of the bride's
parents. As far as the main points are concerned, however, the
report does not deviate greatly from Verschueren's description.
It stresses the passive role of the bride, and even extends this
to the groom, who is said to be as much taken by surprise by his
marriage as his consort.

However that may be, in his description of the marriage procedure Verschueren was preoccupied with other problems. He wrote
his papers on the Yéi-nan as a member of a team investigating the
causes of depopulation among the Marind. It is only natural that
in this context he wanted to contrast the sexual habits of the
Yéi with those of the sex-obsessed Marind. As he had a bent for
forceful expression, the contrast became all too easily a black-
white one, dominated by the notion that the Yéi were better than
the Marind. We are told repeatedly that the Yéi treated their
womenfolk well. It is possible, even probable, that they were
less given to chastising their wives than the Marind, but the
position occupied by their women was decidedly lower than among
the Marind. This becomes clear once we put the facts reported by
Verschueren in the context of their social setting. This context
differs widely from that prevailing among the Marind.

The latter lived in predominantly endogamous villages in which

the youngsters of both sexes had ample opportunity to meet their
future marriage partners, their parents' preference for premarital chastity for the girls and efforts to keep the two sexes
separated notwithstanding. Among the Yéi there was no such kind
of village. Every settlement was strictly exogamous, and potential marriage partners always lived far away in another *arow*.
One look at the map suffices to realize that these distances
were, normally, considerable. This setting favoured a strict control of the sexual behaviour of girls. In the chapter on initiation, data will be put forward which demonstrate how effective
the separation between boys and girls in fact was. This is corroborated by the fact, stated explicitly by Verschueren, that in
the past girls never became pregnant before marriage. His informants emphatically insisted that such a thing was actually impossible, since the social control was too rigorous to provide an
opportunity for this.[3]

In contrast with the Marind, Yéi-nan girls had no say in the
choice of their marriage partner. From the facts as presented by
Verschueren we have to conclude that a girl was always taken to
some far-off, to her foreign, settlement to live with a man whom
she had never met and where she enjoyed no other protection than
that afforded by the community of women there, who were all in
the same position as she. This picture is far too gloomy. Later
(at the end of Chapter VIII) I will have cause to point out that
normally a girl married into a community traditionally related
to her own by connubial relations of long standing. Thus she must
have found herself reunited in her husband's community with classificatory sisters and mothers originating from her own settlement. And she must have seen the men of her husband's group on
the occasion of intercommunal festivities. Perhaps she had even
had contacts with some of them (cf. Section 3 below).

Even so the marriage ceremonies as described above are enlight-
ening. Marriage was a feast of the women, not of the men. The
latter drank kava and fell asleep. But the women did not drink
kava, and (though nothing is said about this) it is almost certain that they went on gossiping among themselves until the small
hours. They first welcomed their new companion, and the next morning the young women would have a merry feast with the newcomer in
what is specifically a women's domain, the sago grove. It constituted an expression of togetherness which, among fellow-sufferers,
is not surprising. It is also an indication that the rigid separation of the sexes in their living quarters entailed so many close
mutual contacts among the women as to give rise to a real women's
community, a rare phenomenon as such. Another sign of the existence of a real community of this kind is the assistance given by
the women to a widow wishing to elope.

This may testify that, in spite of their low legal status, they
did not suffer inconsiderate or rude treatment by their spouses,
who at home could not even reach their wives. Apparently a
woman's life was bearable. An indication to that effect may be
provided by the fact that divorce was decidedly rare. Another
piece of evidence for this may be that the trend among Yéi males
to imitate the Marind has not induced them to adopt the form of

sexual promiscuity known as *otiv bombari*, that is, the copulating
in rapid succession of some six to twelve men with one woman.
Once, on being told that the Marind sometimes perform *otiv bombari* as a means of warding off illness, the Yéi commented: "You
can only become sicker that way".

   With regard to sexual promiscuity Verschueren informs us that
it was practised in two different forms. One was wife exchange
by mutual agreement. Unfortunately we are not told whether the
women also agreed. The other was that of generalized sexual promiscuity on the eve of a headhunt. Then, "the married men, by
mutual agreement, had sexual intercourse with their [probably
"each other's"] wives, after which both the men and women washed
their genitals in a palm-leaf bowl, the contents of which were
later that night sprinkled over the sleeping men by the *gab-elul*,
or war-leader".

   After this digression, let us return to Verschueren's text. It
proceeds with, consecutively, the legal aspects of marriage, the
limited extent of the practice of abortion, and birth and child-
care. These subjects are presented here under the heading "Con-
jugal life".

3. Conjugal life

The Yéi did not treat their wives badly. The one task which the
women had to perform unaided was that of sago pounding. For all
their other tasks they might rely on their husbands for assistance.
The latter, for their part, had a number of jobs in which they
could not expect to be helped by their wives such as the manufacture
of tools and the construction of a canoe.

   In marriage, both spouses retain their personal belongings. The
yields of a garden which they have made together are their common
property, but anything acquired by either of them personally is
his or her own. On her marriage, a wife comes to share her husband's
rights of use to the land and fishing grounds of his group. She will
never try to make sago in the plantations of her own parents, as
this would be grossly offensive to her husband.

   Editor's comment. Of course it would. These gardens are so far
   distant that the act would imply her having run back to her parents. Verschueren's remark is a typical example of his inclina-
   tion to present Yéi-nan matrimonial relations in a somewhat rosy
   light.

Yet, the wife does not acquire any personal right to her husband's
gardens. If he dies, she may continue to exercise these rights if
she has children. If she has none, and if she is not claimed as a
wife by her late husband's brother, she has to return to her own
family. Landed property and claims to fishing-grounds are inherited
in the male line and by males only. A woman's rights inside the
territory of the group to which she has been born terminate with
her marriage. [Undoubtedly they will be revived if, for whatever
reason, she returns to her own descent group.]
   Personal belongings such as tools and ornaments are often given

away well before death. If this has not happened, a man's more valuable belongings, such as an axe, pass to his eldest son. However, the widow usually also receives a proper share.

Notwithstanding the fact that their husbands are fond of children and strongly desire them, the wives of the Yéi-nan sometimes made use of contraceptives. Most of these were of a harmless, purely magical, nature. The most familiar method is that of disposing of the placenta in an abnormal way, such as by burying it under a bamboo stool or in a termite nest, or by wrapping it up in a coconut shell which is thrown into an eddy in the river. Everywhere in these parts the placenta is associated with strong magical powers, and by handling it thus the women hope to ward off or prevent a renewed pregnancy.

   Editor's comment. The performance of this act, which naturally
   follows closely upon the woman's delivery, presupposes the com-
   plicity of at least one other woman. It thus constitutes another
   indication of the solidarity of the female sex.

There were also methods of terminating a pregnancy, some magical, others physical. The magical means included the use of certain leaves, herbs and plants which, by their form or manner of growth, suggest an association with the acts of shrivelling up, shattering, throwing away or tying up. They are all ineffectual. Really efficacious, but often disastrous, are the physical methods, such as tying off or massaging the abdomen, jumping down from a high place and landing on the heels, or lying down on a stone (either previously heated or not) or a coconut. All these methods are well-known but very rarely practised; the women realize altogether too well that the risks are considerable.
   As soon as a woman is visibly pregnant, sexual intercourse is temporarily stopped. In every other respect she follows the usual course of her daily routine. Until the day of her delivery she is not subject to any specific taboos or rites.
   Delivery does not take place in the *wake* but in the nearby bush, where the prospective mother, usually assisted by her mother-in-law, has constructed a simple shed well in advance. Shortly before the labour pains set in, a few older women accompany her to the hut. During the actual delivery little help is given, but the cutting off of the umbilical cord immediately after the birth is performed by one of the senior women. In the case of a boy this must be done by cutting in an upward and of a girl in a downward direction. The cord has prior to this been tied off with tree-bark fibre. It is cut off to a length of only two [?] centimetres. The mother used to stay in the hut for a few days, but she would be back again in the *wake* before the umbilical cord fell off. After the cord had dropped off, the mother would wear it in her ear.
   The baby is washed immediately after birth. Renewed bathing is not allowed for some time. After the delivery the mother and father are subject to a protracted taboo on meat and fish. However, sago-worms, mice, rats, and so forth are allowed.
   If a birth did not pass off normally, a ritual had to be perform-

ed. A woman who fails to give birth is supposed to have been struck by the *yevale* (spirit) Baderam. Some older women seat themselves around the woman in labour, who must now tell them the names of all the men and boys other than her husband with whom she has had sexual intercourse, either since the days of her youth or since her last confinement. [These questions throw considerable doubt on the claims about premarital chastity; see page 30.] Then one of the older women takes a croton twig and asks the patient whether these are really all, whether she has not forgotten or withheld any name. She then brushes the twig over the patient's body from head to feet, muttering: *"Uke, tjuke gei tir, uke tjuke wale tir, uke tjuke matatnéam tir, uke tjuke ka ketsyon tir, uke tjuke u tir, uke tjuke töttu tir"*, i.e., "Tear out the talons of the harrier, the talons of the *ndamau*, the talons of the male bird of paradise, of the black evening-bird, of the morning-bird". The formula refers to the talons of the harrier (*gei tir*) and of other birds which women as well as men used to wear through the perforations in the wings of their nose. In explanation of the formula informants said that Baderam has grasped the woman's neck and is now entreated to let go of her, whatever the talons (*tir*) by which she has grasped her. Comparing this ceremony with that of *nakyasub* (see Chapter VI), ceremonies which are also associated with Baderam, the supposition that Baderam is the cause of pregnancy forces itself upon us (cf. the myth). What results from it in this case is a child, in that of *nakyasub*, a *sinak* (woman's apron).[4]

Four or fives days after her delivery the young mother blackens her body (*not* that of the baby) with charcoal and returns to her old place in the *wake*. So far the father has not seen the baby, and he does not try to look at it even now. He painstakingly keeps aloof, officially because he is ashamed. In reality he keeps aloof, as all the men do, because they might harm the baby. A *yevale* might be hiding among them and hurt the child. It is for this same reason that, if a member of another group enters the *soama*, a bamboo torch is beaten on the ground in front of the visitor's feet, in order to chase away the *yevale* of any other, hostile *jéi* which might be accompanying him.

Once the infant is able to sit, it is given a name. The name-giver is the father, and the name bestowed on the child is usually that of the father's father or mother, or of one of the father's siblings. Later the father may exchange the name with another one, usually because the child is suffering from an illness ascribed to a *yevale*. It is hoped that the child will thus escape the *yevale*'s influence. At a more mature age children may adopt a self-chosen name. Name-giving is *not* associated with changes in age-grade. Head-names, taken from victims beheaded on a war raid, are not prevalent among the Yéi, though the southern villages, in imitation of the Marind, sometimes make an exception.

Twins are not killed, not even one of such twins. Apparently, a twin-birth is not considered magically dangerous. Usually, the parents keep one child for themselves and give the other away in adoption to some other couple.

The *bogu*, the taboo on meat [and fish?] to which the parents have submitted at the child's birth, is observed, not, as among the

Marind, until the reappearance of the menses, but - reportedly -
often until the child is able to walk or even to talk. Much depends
upon the child. It must be able to participate in the consumption
of the meat by the parents on the occasion of their discarding the
taboo. Accustoming the child to solid food is a long-drawn process.
At the age of four or five months this begins with mature bananas,
later followed by roasted bananas. Little by little the child is
familiarized with yams, taro, and finally sago, in that sequence.
This does not mean that the process of suckling comes to an end.
Weaning does not take place until the next pregnancy, and if this
is not forthcoming, suckling may continue for several years.

> *Editor's comment.* The teachers' papers provide a slightly differ-
> ent picture. They tell us that a father joins his wife immediate-
> ly after her delivery, and stays with her in the hut until the
> time he is able to escort her and the baby back to their home.
> They also state that the food taboos imposed on both parents are
> very strict until the time the umbilical cord has dropped off,
> and even include a prohibition on drinking water. Once the above
> event has taken place the taboos become milder. They are of con-
> siderably shorter duration than Verschueren suggests. Probably
> these differences reflect changes from old-time customs (which
> enjoyed Verschueren's special interest) to the more modern prac-
> tice of 1934, the year in which the teachers wrote their papers.
> In this context also figure 2 of plate I is of interest. The
> artist, the Mission teacher Renwarin, tells us that the two ob-
> jects are a coconut half and a carved wooden object suspended
> near an infant's cradle to protect it against spirits and *yevale*
> (he uses the term *dema*), who take fright when they see these
> objects. Obviously, the carved wooden object is a *kupör*, or bull-
> roarer, here represented in the form of a spatula.

When the parents feel that their child is old enough to eat meat,
the father takes his bow and arrows and goes into the forest to
shoot a bird, a scrub-hen or a Goura pigeon. The first shot must
not miss its mark, lest the child become troublesome and fretful.
If the first bird shot is a *beroga* [scrub-hen?], the man will not
kill it on the spot but will bring it alive to his wife for her to
twist the bird's neck. The *beroga* is a noisy fellow and might turn
the child into a cry-baby and a whiner. Together with their child,
the husband and wife now eat meat again for the first time. The
taboo is, indeed, protracted and demanding, though it is not as
rigorously observed as is often suggested. The parents are allowed
to participate in the eating of meat or game killed by someone else
if they happen to be present when the meat is roasted.
  The discarding of the taboo is not accompanied by any form of
ceremony. The husband and wife unobtrusively return to the normal
routine of their married life. The father is now allowed to take
the child in his arms, something hitherto forbidden to him. Informants pointed out that formerly unmarried people were not allowed
to embrace a child, because this would have adverse sexual effects.
  During their first years children, boys as well as girls, stay
with their mother. In the house they are allowed to go wherever

they wish. The invisible division of the house into a men's and a
women's quarter has no consequences for them before puberty. During
the day they accompany their mothers and grandmothers to the gardens and swamps, unless they are left behind under the care of some
old woman. In the house there is no real family life. This has its
proper setting in the gardens or sago groves.

Women and girls were not allowed to leave the house alone, but
had to be accompanied by a mother-in-law or another woman. A husband who wished to go with his wife to their garden usually informed her of his intentions through his mother; this was the most
practical way, because older men and women occupy the central part
of the house. Food, too, was usually transmitted through the medium
of an older woman.

Events which, among the Marind-anim, provided an occasion for a
small family celebration - the piercing of the earlobes or the
nasal septum, for instance - used to take place without any celebration at all, unless they coincided with some other festive
occasion. Ordinarily, such operations were performed at a very
early age.

Editor's comment. Mr. Renwarin, the mission teacher of Kekayu
(Polka), tells us that there it was customary to celebrate the
piercing of the earlobes with a feast organized by the combined
parents of all the children, boys and girls, between 7 and 10
years of age. Guests were invited from everywhere in the sur-
roundingaareas. The night following their arrival was passed in
singing (and dancing) *bendol*. At daybreak the children were assembled near a big pile of garden produce (*inter alia* yams, taro
and kava) topped with two bagsful of sago. They were seated on
top of the heap one after the other to have their earlobes pierc-
ed by their respective mothers' brothers. Finally, the garden
produce was distributed among the guests.

Verschueren must have known about this kind of celebration but
probably omitted to make mention of it because, to him, it was
not originally Yéi but just another imitation of the Marind. The
procedure as described by Renwarin does, in fact, point in that
direction.

Chapter IV

The Founding Myths of Yéi-nan Ritual

1. Editor's introduction

Verschueren's accounts of Yéi-nan myth and ritual abound with
references to his dispute with Wirz and Nevermann about the presence of totemism among the Yéi, and about their identification
of the *yevale* with ancestors. In this dispute he went to the
extent of denying the presence of any form of totemism among the
Yéi, except where this had been borrowed from the Marind. In this
he was decidedly wrong; his own data prove that totemism constituted part of their tradition. However - and here he was right -
it was a form of totemism which differed widely from the cult
totemism of the Marind which, combined as it is with multiple
totemism and an elaborate ancestor cult, is of the Australian
type. The totemism of the Yéi is more like that of the Keraki as
described by Williams, and that of the Kiwai as we know it from
the works of Landtman. It is a kind of totemism with hardly any
ritual implications. Unfortunately, Verschueren was not an anthropologist and was not familiar with any of these books.

His opinion that the *yevale* are *not* ancestors, and certainly
not ancestors of the type of the Marind-anim *dema*, is better
founded, though at times doubts about this arise. Many *yevale* are
localized spirits who stand in a certain relation to a particular
local *jéi* and can be invoked by its members. However, the myths
related in Chapter IX depict them as a kind of spirits which are
more akin to those of Landtman's Folktales than to the Marind-
anim *dema*. The few examples we came across in Section 3 of the
previous chapter, as well as those we shall find in Chapter VIII,
point in the same direction. The Yéi are always on their guard
against the *yevale*, who, more often than not, are harbingers of
evil. Actually, there is only one weak point in Verschueren's
argument for refusing to classify the *yevale* with ancestors: the
few times he speaks of the Yéi-nan ancestors he omits to mention
the native term by which they are designated by his informants.
Nevertheless, this can hardly be a reason for not placing in him
the confidence which he deserves as a gifted and dedicated observer. The less so because the data furnished by him form a consistent and coherent whole. They confront us with an out-and-out
phallic cult of which Verschueren himself had not even an inkling.
Under these circumstances we are well advised to take him at his
word.

Two errors barred his way to a correct understanding of his
mythical material. The one is his underestimation of the significance of headhunting in Yéi-nan culture as a result of his regarding them (like so many others) as victims rather than as agents

of the practice. Nevertheless, the fact that the Yéi preserve
not only the skulls but also the long bones of their victims and
arrange these into a kind of still-life displayed on the central
pole of the communal house - the Yéi are wholly unique in this
respect - should have warned him that there was more to it.

His second error was the result of his being confused by the
fact that the Yéi have two main myths of origin. His conclusion
was that there are two mythical cycles, the one social and the
other magico-religious, and he treated these separately, the one
(the cycle concerned with Ndiwe, Nak and Telle) in the context
of the origin of the clans and moieties, the other in that of
magic and religion, disregarding the fact that this second "cycle"
is not really a cycle. It begins with one important myth, the
myth of the *orei* tree, which has little to do with the other
"religious" myths, which are relegated here to Chapter IX. The
myth of the *orei* tree, however, is given a place in this chapter,
not because it stands in contrast to the myths of Ndiwe, Nak and
Telle, but because it forms their complement. The reasons for
this will become apparent in due course.

2. The myth of Ndiwe

Like the upper Bian people and the Boadzi, the Yéi assume that they
did not originate in their present area of residence. Together with
the Boadzi, the upper Bian Marind, the Aroba [a Suki group?] and
the Kanum, they owe their existence to Ndiwe, the demiurge who
among all these tribes plays the role of originator. Ndiwe (also
called Ndiwa or Nggiwe) is not a creator, but rather an improver
who brings the shape of man to perfection and gives him his social
institutions. Before Ndiwe's intervention the upper Bian Marind had
no females, the Boadzi lived underground as pigs and the Aroba were
cassowaries at the mercy of a malignant supreme being. The Yéi, for
their part, lived somewhere in the middle Fly region[1] in a subterra-
nean hole, together with the other "nations" just mentioned. None
of them had either mouths or noses, eyes or ears. It was Ndiwe who,
by cutting them open, finished their human shape. They immediately
started talking. Ndiwe listened. Hearing their speech, he said to
some of them: "You are upper Bian Marind", to others: "You are
Boadzi", while others again he called Yéi, and finally there were
those whom he called Kanum. He then divided them into groups and
escorted them one by one to the country where they belonged: the
Marind to the upper Bian, the Boadzi to the upper Fly, and the Yéi-
nan to the Maro.

In a more detailed version we are told that Ndiwe came from the
east or northeast [the three documents are not consonant on this
point]. He came from the middle Fly, and was accompanied by his
old mother. He brought the ancestors of the Yéi. They entered the
Maro region at Karopo, a place on the upper Bárkí River, east of
the heart of the present-day Yéi-nan territory. Arriving on the
Burrau (the Maro River), they discovered the territory to be occupied by other people. But Ndiwe commanded: "These people do not
belong here. We must chase them away; so we must fight them".
(According to an alternative version, told at Kwél, the Burrau did

not yet exist at that time. It came into being after the first occupants had been expelled.)

The ancestors who followed Ndiwe did not have any personal names.
Ndiwe now gave each of the men his proper name, at the same time
handing him a *kupe*, a disc-shaped stone with a hole in the centre.
Through this hole a stout stick, usually a rattan one, may be passed, making the whole thing into a club, the formidable weapon of
the Yéi. But the stones may be of various kinds. Besides the disc-
shaped stones, the *kupe* proper, there are also egg-shaped ones
(*bawa*) and stones that are notched (*giri-giri*). They all serve the
same purpose, and the term *kupe* can be used for all of them.

Editor's comment. The *kupe* may also be placed on the *pöggul*, the
ceremonial staff (and club) of the *gab-elul* (headman) described
in Section 2 of Chapter II. The *pöggul* is the exact counterpart
of the Marind *pahui*, described and discussed in Van Baal 1966:
617ff., 662f., and 730-43 as one of the latter's most important
ritual attributes. Among the Marind the disc-shaped stone (*kupa*)
is a female symbol, the egg-shaped one (*wagané*; Yéi: *bawa*) a male
one (Van Baal 1966:273). On their use as parts of the *pahui* (Yéi:
pöggul) and their possible association with each of the two moieties see Van Baal 1966 Chapter XII, in particular p. 742. It is
not impossible that the Yéi made a similar distinction, equipping
the Nak with a *bawa* and the Telle with a *kupe* for their *pöggul*.
Unfortunately, this must remain hypothetical.

Another interesting character in this context is the old mother
who accompanies Ndiwe on his peregrinations in the territory of
the Yéi. She plays an important part in Boadzi myth and ritual,
notably in the ritual surrounding headhunting. What is more, she
is identified with the stone disc on the *pahui* of the Boadzi, an
association which is in perfect harmony with her place in the
present story. For relevant literature see Van Baal 1966:590-7,
726ff., and in particular 730.

Ndiwe, then, handed such a stone to each of his companions, simul-
taneously defining the receiver's identity by bestowing a personal
name on him, viz. *Kupe gön, bu Dambu ... Kupe gön, bu Kello* ("Here
is a *kupe*, you are Dambu ... you are Kello"), etc.[2] And this, the
Yéi will add, was the origin of the *jéi*. [Note that Dambu and Kelle
are *jéi* names!]

But Ndiwe did more. According to an informant from Kwél, Ndiwe
had kept behind two *kupe* passed over a shaft topped by a beautifully carved fretwork blade. Once everyone had received a *kupe*, Ndiwe
let the men run a race. The two winners were Nak and Telle. Each
of them received one of these beautiful ceremonial clubs, *pöggul*,
and thus became the first *gab-elul*, war-leaders, of the Yéi-nan.

Now fighting broke out. They first expelled the people of the
southerly area and chased them down the Maro River to beyond Tayas.
Then they returned to drive out the occupants of the upper reaches
of the river and chased them to the Kumbe and the Bian. On their
flight the Northerners left their drums behind, which were taken by
Ndiwe and his men. Then Ndiwe said: "Now this is your country", and
he gave each of the ancestors a territory of his own. These ances-

tors then took their *kupe* and everyone laid his *kupe* down in the
centre of his own territory. And this division of the land into *jéi*
territories has persisted until the present day. After the division
of the available land among the *jéi*, a big feast was held at Gelel,
a place near Benóong [exact location unknown]. (According to an alternative version from Bupul the Yéi-nan originated here, in Gelel,
during the celebration. They emerged one by one from a hole in the
ground.)

The story testifies that the *jéi* originated as territorial groups,
and that their names are those of their ancestors [cf. above and
note 2], which names sometimes do and sometimes do not have a meaning in the Yéi language. There is no question of any totemic relation, however. Down to the present day the *jéi*-stones are still kept
where they were laid down, each in its own territory. They are called *komen*, in order to distinguish them explicitly from other stones
and objects which spring from the *yevale* themselves and will be discussed later [which promise remained unfulfilled]. These *komen* are
deeply revered but not worshipped. They are simply designated the
"heart" or "navel" of the territory.

[In ms. C the data on the *komen* are summarized as follows: The
ancestors laid down their *kupe* as the navel of their property in the
centre of the territory assigned to them. Their descendants, who
have adopted the name of their ancestor as the name of their group,
consider the still treasured *kupe* as the centre of their inherited
territory. These stones, *komen*, are reverently preserved but not
worshipped, unless, as is quite often the case, they have been
chosen by *yevale* for their abode.]

Editor's comment. The passage just quoted from ms. C is of interest because it gives substance to the distinction made between
reverence and worship. Evidently, there is no question of ritual
taking place at the location of the *komen* unless it is at the
same time the residence of a *yevale*. The same idea is expressed
in the curious passage introducing the account of the myth of
Ndiwe in ms. B, a passage which we have passed over in silence
because it contains a few elements which, in an introductory statement, would have a confusing rather than an elucidating effect.
The passage, which is more in place here, runs as follows:
"As has already been noted by Wirz, the entire *jéi* system is
focused on a stone of the most fantastic form. Every *jéi*, as a
territorial group, has somewhere in its territory, on some spit
of land or other - sometimes in a coconut garden, then again in
a clearing in a dark forest, in a bamboo grove, or simply in the
centre of an open plain - a stone which is guarded with every
sign of respect. The ground around the stone is kept scrupulously
clean, and croton shrubs are planted around it, with one or more
hardwood poles added. These stones are called *komen*; they are
the permanent property of the local *jéi* and are deeply respected."
However, as even Wirz admitted: "Der Schwerpunkt liegt nicht so-
sehr in dem Naturobjekt aber im Jewale, dasz er unter Umständen
darstellt" (i.e., It is not so much the natural object as the
yevale occasionally represented by it that matters) (Wirz 1925
(III):202).[3]

Although the quotation is incorrect and out of place - as Wirz said this not of the *komen* but of the totems which he believed to be associated with the *yevale* - the author's intention is evident: the place derives its ritual importance from the occasional presence of a *yevale*. The description of its outward appearance is intriguing. Why are one or more hardwood poles planted here? The answer is not too difficult. What can they represent but the shaft of the club or *pöggul* from which the ancestors took their *kupe* when, on their return from the campaign against the foreign occupants of their territory, they put it down at the navel of their newly acquired territory? It is a tempting thesis, reminiscent of the procedure, described later on in this chapter (Section 7), whereby a returning war party pay their respects to the *arow yevale*, where the *gab-elul* then plants the shaft of his *pöggul* after taking off its *kupe* (the fretwork blade having already disappeared in the battle).

It is a hypothesis to which we shall have to return later. Here another problem demands our attention. It is raised by Verschueren's description of the *komen* as stones of the most fantastic shape, while at the same time assuring us that they are *kupe*. He does not explain the discrepancy. Apparently we must assume that the Yéi, in the firm conviction that their *komen are* the one-time *kupe* of their ancestors, did not bother too much about such deviations in form. They were once *kupe*, and in things religious this is enough. Nevertheless, further inquiry into this matter teaches us that the Yéi were not as indifferent on this point as Verschueren's rather haphazard description suggests. Wirz, too, has seen these stones and has given a short description of five of them. Two were stones of the size of a human head (III:204), the third was a real *kupe* (III:207), the fourth was a stone with an artificially incised groove, suggesting its former use in grinding axestones, and the fifth again a *kupe*, but this time with an unfinished hole (both p. 208).

3. The myths of Nak and Telle

[The mythical account of the exploits of the ancestors was broken off at the point where they met at Gelel to hold a big feast. From now on no more mention is made of Ndiwe. After having divided the people into clans and moieties and distributed land and *kupe* among them, he fades out of the story.]

The feast at Gelel was a glorious feast, but it ended in chaos, as a result of the crime committed by Belám, a Marind man of the Kumbe River who, with his wife Genggen and their baby daughter, lived in the bush not far from Gelel.

Every day Genggen went to the nearby swamp to catch fish, leaving Belám alone with their little daughter. Belám was working on a new drum, which would bear his own name, Belám. However, he also had to take care of the child. It was so young that it was still lying in a cradle. This caused him a great deal of trouble and vexation. When his wife stayed away too long, this irritated him. Nevertheless, she brought home fish and sago, and thus he controlled himself and kept quiet. In the long run, the constantly returning bur-

den of having to look after the child became too much for him, the
more so because he heard the sounds of the dancing and singing of
the merry-makers at Gelel every night. His drum was almost finished
and, putting the final touches to his work, he sang: *Oh, oh, oh,
Belám ah, Gelel ago ah.* But the child started crying again. It
drove Belám out of his mind. Suddenly he arose, took the baby,
cradle and all, and threw it into the fire, where everything burned
to ashes. He then took his drum and hurried off to Gelel, where he
was jostled into the centre of the crowd of dancers, so that his
wife would not be able to find him.

On coming home, Genggen soon discovered what had happened. She
was furious. She fastened the sharp nails of a cassowary to her fingers and toes and tried them out on a banana stem. They passed right
through. She now turned herself into a lean dog and went to Gelel
in search of her husband. All over the feasting-ground she sniffed
at the legs of the dancers, who, in their irritation, kicked her
off, wondering who the owner of that lean dog could be. But Genggen
did not give up till she became tired and lay down on a rubbish-
heap to sleep. The second day she was more successful. She managed
to penetrate into the inner ring of dancers and there, indeed, found
Belám dancing. She straightaway started biting and scratching at
his body with her cassowary nails. Belám screamed and cried so loud-
ly that all the dancers took a tremendous fright and ran off, back
to their country, without so much as thinking about their possessions. Nak and Telle, too, ran off and did not come to rest until they reached the Obat River, where they had their domains on
opposite sides of the river. (According to an alternative version
Telle fled alone to his house and Nak followed him later.) On their
flight each of them had salvaged at least some of his possessions,
Nak the fire and his bow and arrows, Telle the sago.

Nak and Telle were friends, and even more than friends: they were
men of the same age, *yát.* Consequently Nak invited Telle to go
hunting on one of the elevated spits of land on his side of the
river. "Let us go hunting, *yát*", said Nak. "All right, but how will
I catch any game?" asked Telle, because he did not have a bow. And
Nak answered: "You just throw a stick at the game". Telle replied:
"All right. You stay here and wait and I shall run around the hill
and drive the game in your direction". He collected a couple of
sticks and then took off. He did not know that Nak had a bow and
arrows, nor that he had concealed them in a hollow tree. As soon
as Telle had left, Nak took them out and without any difficulty
shot a cassowary and a wallaby. He put his bow and arrows back in
their hiding-place, and painted a couple of sticks with the blood
of the animals he had killed. When Telle turned up, breathless and
empty-handed, he praised Nak's dexterity. "Yes", said Nak, "I aimed
carefully and hit them in the right spot". Then he fairly divided
the catch, and Telle returned to his own territory.

Nak secretly made a fire, singed the hair off his catch and roasted the meat. But Telle had to eat his meat raw, with hide and hair.
Fortunately he had sago which he mixed with the raw meat, whereas
Nak had to make do with sand for a side-dish. Consequently Nak's
teeth wore down unevenly, and more and more came to resemble those
of a wallaby.

Whenever Nak and Telle hunted together, the same thing happened
all over again. At last Telle became suspicious. He thought: "Why
is it that Nak always catches the game and that he eats of it so
well?" He asked Nak about it, who answered: "Well, I always aim
very carefully at the head of the animal. That is where you must
hit them. And the meat, well, it is dry because I expose it to the
sun for some time." But Telle was on the alert. One day he received
a portion of meat with part of an arrow in it which had broken off
on striking the bone. Besides, part of the hide had been scorched
by fire. "Ah, that's it!", he thought, *ukulede kene gen, ban kane
gen* [translation lacking]. He said to Nak: "*Yât!* Let us go hunting
again; and this time I want to go a long, long way. When you no
longer hear me calling, you will know that I am far off." Before-
hand he had decorated a pole in such a way that, from afar, it re-
sembled a man wearing a headdress of cassowary and bird of paradise
feathers. He made off, now and then running very fast, and finally
disappeared in the bush, to return in secret to the place where he
had left Nak. The latter had been scanning the plain, and had sight-
ed the feathered pole. He smiled and went to the hollow tree to
fetch his bow and arrows [and, according to another version, the
fire]. Telle, who had seen where he kept them, hurried off in search
of game. When he finally returned, Nak had already shot a few animals. Telle was empty-handed, and complained: "I never catch anything!" Again Nak explained that he should try to hit the head,
and Telle replied: "Indeed, I should throw better. Perhaps I would
do better if you, *yât*, did the driving and I stayed here and waited."
Nak agreed and made off, but hardly had he disappeared when Telle
took the fire, the bow and the arrows from the hollow tree and
hurried back home. He set the savannah afire to let Nak have his
part of the fire, but kept the "head" of the fire for himself. In
the meantime Nak ran after him. As the grass-fire went out, he over-
took Telle at Kíndél, on the Palwa River. But they did not fight.
They were *yât*. Nak praised Telle for his shrewdness and taught him
how to make a bow and arrows for himself. In return, Telle filed
Nak's long teeth until they were as neat and even as his own.
   The story of the fire and the bow is sometimes combined with that
of the sago, Telle giving sago in exchange for Nak's bow. Another
alternative version is the following: Nak asked Telle how he kept
his teeth so nice and even. Wishing to keep his possession of sago
a secret, Telle answered: "By adding mud to the sand which I eat
with my meat". Nak tried this out, but the mud stuck to his palate
and he realized that Telle had tricked him. The next time that they
had hunted together, he secretly followed Telle on his way home and
saw how Telle took sago from a bag, and mixed it with the meat which
he had brought home. Now Nak had taken his two trained red cockatoos
with him. He ordered them to perch on the banana trees near Telle's
house, and there make all the noise they could. They did this, and
Telle immediately jumped to his feet to run after the cockatoos.
Meanwhile Nak snatched the bag with sago and ran off. Telle happened by accident to look over his shoulder, and immediately realized
that he had been outwitted by Nak. Smiling, he returned, and said:
"*Yât*, you found it", and taught him the technique of sago-making.
   The two red cockatoos also play a role in a variant version of

the story of the fire which was told in Erambu. Telle had noticed
that Nak was burning his garden site. He wished to get hold of the
fire but could not come near enough, because the two cockatoos
warned their master as soon as anyone approached. So he asked a *po
mermer* (lizard) clinging to a coconut tree to steal the fire for
him. But the *po mermer* could not carry it. Then he appealed to a
bengkaron, a somewhat larger lizard with a tilted head, but the
bengkaron refused. Finally, he asked the small *dagole* lizard, this
time successfully so. Unfortunately, the firebrand was too large
and the *dagole* burned its chest. And this is why the *dagole* has a
red spot on its breast up to the present day. In return for the
fire Telle taught Nak everything about the sago.

The exchange motif recurs in the story of how Telle taught Nak
to build a house. Telle had a house roofed with sago leaves; Nak
slept under a large tree. Telle told Nak how to construct a house,
but Nak complained that he had no sago-trees there. "Then take
eucalyptus bark", Telle answered, and explained how to cut the bark
with a shell. He sat down, giving instructions, and Nak did the
work. When Nak had finished his house, they were both happy, Telle
because of the bow and arrows, Nak because of his house. And each
of them stayed in his own house.

There are lots of stories about Nak and Telle. One of these
relates how Nak terrified Telle by beating a drum which he had secretly manufactured. But the most instructive of all these stories
are those about their making a fish-trap together.

One day Nak said: "*Yát*, you should come here to fish. The water
is dropping. On your side of the river there is only bush, and the
fish are scarce there". As it happened, Nak had erected a weir
in the [small] river. On one side of this he had placed a number of
fish-traps (*bubus*). When they came to the river bank, Nak said to
Telle: "We must dive here. Each of us will take a strip of rattan
with him. If you see a fish, then wait till it opens its gills. If
you are quick, you will be able to thrust the strip through them."
He pointed out where Telle should dive (on the side without the
fish-traps), and they both descended. Nak swiftly emptied his traps
and emerged with his rattan strip full of fish. But Telle, in spite
of all his efforts, caught no more than only one single fish. Back
on the river bank, they collected their catch and divided it into
two equal portions, because they were *yát*. But Nak mocked Telle,
saying: "You are just like a small boy with that tiny little fish
of yours".

Telle, well aware that Nak had tricked him once again, kept
silent. The next morning he hid himself near the weir and saw
how Nak pulled up his fish-traps, well filled with fish, and then
placed the traps on a fallen tree to dry them in the sun. And toward evening he noticed Nak tying up the open ends of the traps and
placing them back again into the holes in the barrier under the
water. The next morning, before dawn, Telle emptied the traps. He
tied the fish to a rattan strip and hid everything under the water
on his side of the barrier. Putting on an innocent face, he now
went to Nak and proposed going fishing once more. This they did.
Telle emerged with his rattan full of fish and Nak empty-handed,
because Telle had forgotten to tie up the open ends of the traps

after clearing them. Nak was furious. Back on the river bank, they fought, Nak beating Telle with a fish-trap and Telle thrashing Nak with the fishes. Then they made peace, and Nak told Telle how to make and use a fishing-weir. He promised to come to Telle's side of the river to help him construct one for himself.

So they worked together on a new barrier. Nak descended into the river to stop the barrier with sago leaves which Telle, standing on the upper edge of the barrier, handed to him. Now Telle was actually a woman, though he was wearing a penis shell. Nak emerged from the water, saying: "I am getting cold. I think it is your turn to descend." Saying this, he looked up and saw something really startling. He cried out: *Mugu gen bu, Elisame, Kamé Kamé!*: "You are of the Mugu-*jéi*, of the Elisame, of the Kamé *jéi!*" All three are Telle *jéi*. And from this moment on he refused to call Telle *yát*. Yet they finished the fish-weir and made a fire. Then they inspected the fish-traps and collected an enormous amount of fish. Telle fetched firewood and *nibung*-spathes with which to roast the fish, and Nak brought kava from his garden. That night Nak brewed a really potent kava drink for Telle. He himself took only a small sip. Telle got completely drunk, but Nak took a torch and inspected Telle's genitals. That night he made her his wife. He gave her a *sinak* (women's apron) and said: "You must discard your *possé* (penis shell) because from now on you are my wife".

Finally [this is added in a note], there is a last alternative version which tells how Nak and Telle came to blows near a fish-trap and then changed into a *nak* (= fish-eagle) and a *telle* (= hen-harrier).

Editor's comment. There could be no better proof of totemism among the Yéi than precisely this last addition to the myths about Nak and Telle, made more or less as an afterthought. Only here do we learn that their names are the names of birds of prey, a fish-eagle and a hen-harrier. The pair finds an exact parallel in the moiety totems of the Keraki, about which F.E. Williams wrote: "We may first briefly consider the hawks, which alone find a wide and more or less consistent distribution as totems for the two moieties. The two principal species which are commonly acknowledged by Bangu and Sangara respectively (the two moieties) are *wana* ... and *inifiak* ... The former is the large brown kite with white breast which hunts for snakes and bandicoots; the latter is a somewhat smaller white-headed hawk" (Williams 1936: 89). We shall not attempt an exact identification of the two birds concerned. Geurtjens (*Woordenboek* pp. 406-7) identifies the *nak* and *telle* (spelt *tale* by him) with the *kidub* and *kéké* of the Marind, i.e. the fish-eagle and the hawk. The scientific names are not as important as the question of why Verschueren never gave a thought to the fact, altogether too familiar to him, that his heroes bear birds' names. The answer is that he was too much engrossed in their human traits, which led him to make the following comment:

1. The most obvious feature of the stories of this cycle is that they are concerned with ordinary human beings. They do not bear the

marks of a "sacred history", but are purely human tales which mirror
the relations of dependence prevailing between the two moieties as
well as between husband and wife. That Nak is the male and Telle
the female is not borne out by the scene on the fishing-barrier
alone; it is reflected throughout the whole cycle. Nak is a fisher-
man and possesses such male articles as a bow and arrows, fire and
drum, whereas Telle has sago and a house. The stories are an example of how a husband and wife should supplement one another, forming a dualism based on true friendship and togetherness, which time
and again lapses into the comical conflicts arising from good-
natured trickery. The story as a whole is a gem reflecting deeply
human, psychologically well observed relations in which the recur-
ring tensions are ultimately reconciled to give substance to their
unity.

2. The myths reflect the ideal relation between the moieties. The
one needs the other, and not merely because of the marriage system.
On every occasion of social importance the other moiety is invited
as the indispensable complement. Big hunting and fishing parties
require the cooperation of members of both moieties. At the celebration of a marriage the young women (all of the bride's moiety)
assist the newly wed in making a new sago garden which, ultimately,
will be the property of the husband and his moiety. At a pig-feast
it is not the feast-givers who eat the pigs, but the guests of the
other moiety. At the inauguration of a newly finished canoe, others,
the members of the opposite moiety, must test the new dug-out.

3. The playful element characterizing the adventures of Nak and
Telle plays a comparable role in all celebrations. At the end of a
pig-feast, when the raisers of the pigs receive their share of the
meat, they find themselves suddenly drenched with water poured over
them by their guests to the boisterous hilarity of all those present. Something similar befalls the male guests who, on behalf of
their hosts, pull a newly finished canoe to the river bank. They
will suddenly find hot embers on their path, be besprinkled with
stinging ants, and be made the butt of other such jokes. Even the
mourning ritual has its playful elements. A few days after a mature
man's death, the wives of the deceased's in-laws [i.e. his classificatory sisters!] present pantomimes portraying past events and
exploits in which the deceased has had a hand. The women are dress-
ed up as males, and their travesty, combined with their clumsy imi-
tations of male behaviour, are a source of mild amusement.

4. The question arises whether and to what extent this notion of
complementary dualism can be extended to the homosexual relations
between a boy and his pederast. True enough, he is always a member
of his own exogamous moiety. Men of the other moiety live too far
off to be able to participate in the daily guidance of the boy. Yet,
if we consider the boys as girls in disguise, their role reflects
that of Telle in the myth establishing the institution of moiety
dualism. She was a woman in the guise of a man, a brother who became a wife. The travesty motif is clearly present in the episode
relating how Telle filed Nak's teeth. Nak had to lie down on the
ground with Telle sitting on top of him.

4. The myth of the orei-tree

Editor's introduction. The myth of the *orei*-tree explains the
origin of the *yevale*. There are various myths of this category,
says Verschueren, but they all agree on the point that all *yevale*
"originated from the *orei*-tree (magic palm) ... (and) came to the
country in an *orei*-canoe which was made from that tree. And they
all took a chip of the *orei*-tree with them as a magical implement
(the *kupör* or bullroarer). At the end of their peregrinations
they all disappeared into the ground ..."
   The elaborate version of the myth presented by Verschueren is
the one related in the southern part of the Yéi territory. "It
betrays relations with the Kanum as well as a certain influence
of the Marind", he adds. However, I must confess that I have not
been able to discover what these specific Marind-anim influences
can have been in this myth, unless the author means - as is practically certain - that the myth bears clear traces of totemism,
just like the story of Nak and Telle. That these traces of totemism go back to Keraki (and allied) forms of totemism rather than
to Marind-anim influence need not be argued again.

A large *orei*-tree (a wild areca palm) stood somewhere in Elijéi, in
the open plain formed by the delta of the confluence of the Maro
and Wanggo rivers. Once upon a time all the *yevale* of the Boadzi,
the Marind and the Yéi had assembled here. But the Kanum were absent. The tree stood inside the territory of the Aroba, a small
tribe usually classified with the yam-eating Kanum. Every night
the neighbouring Kanum heard the sound of singing and dancing. They
did not know where the sound came from. They went in search, and
finally came near the *orei*-tree. But every time they came near, all
the occupants of the tree entered their tree through a hole, and
all the Kanum were able to discover were the traces of a celebration.
   One of the Kanum men hid near the tree and listened. After some
time he heard the sound of people inside the *orei*-tree. He went
home and told his tribal fellows: "They are lodged inside the hollow
orei-tree". He went to fetch rattan from the forest to tie his stone
axe to its shaft, because he wished to cut down the *orei*-tree. In
the meantime the *yevale* had come out again and were dancing, but
as soon as the man with the axe appeared, they ran back and crowded
into the hollow tree. The Kanum man took his axe and gave the tree
a hard blow. The tree was hollow and its bark very thin. The axe
struck one of the tree-*yevale* on the forehead, and this is why some
people suffer from headaches.
   But the *orei*-tree fell apart, and all the *yevale* came tumbling
out. Each of the *yevale* took a chip of the tree and took it to his
own country; these became the *kupör*, the bullroarer-like or spatula-
like objects used in all forms of magic. And the wood-cutter took
fright and ran off to his house to tell his people what had happened.
   The *orei*-tree had fallen to pieces, and each of these pieces constituted a canoe, in which the *yevale* went to their country. The
Yéi-*yevale* had their own canoe, and so had the Boadzi and the

Marind. They all went their own way.

But Orei made all his men, the Yéi-*yevale*, enter his canoe
(Kwar).[4] The canoe was full to the brim because, in addition to
the *yevale*, everything had been loaded into it that is typical of
the Obat River region. This included a slim hardwood palmtree, loam,
mud, sago, wild kapok, bamboo, and pandan trees. They put off. Orei
had pushed off his canoe with a certain kind of nibung, and now
wished to change it for a bamboo. But the nibung fell from the
canoe, and this is why nibung trees abound near the mouth of the
Obat. Then he began to scrape the ringworm scales off his body.
Where he threw them away at the mouth of the river's tributaries,
they turned into sago. The canoe was overloaded, and so he put a
yevale ashore at every tributary. At the mouth of the Jármu, Korew
was disembarked, at the Wuj River, Kupale, Godye was put ashore at
the Waimon, and Tsakwe at the Tawái. And each of the *yevale* was
given his *kupör* to take with him.

At the Sembe, Orei set Jögwul down, and gave him his *kupör* in
token of his authority there. At the Yelma, Paltye and Mub were
disembarked. The one is the *yevale* of the earth-hog [echidna?], the
other of the fish called *ikan saku* in Indonesian. Kworeo, the *ikan
duri* (Indonesian, meaning thorny fish), was set down here too, because, as Orei said, we are still far too many in the canoe. In
Mamter he put Balgo, the *yevale* of Yoakema, ashore. With Balgo,
Dedegiam also left the canoe. And at Wanggepo he set Widi down.

When they arrived at the Yób River, Orei began to cut down a
tree (Indonesian name: *pohon susu*). It was meant to fall across the
Yób River. A friend of his by name of Wolpaka wanted to help him.
Orei had concealed the rattan strip by which he had tied his axe
to its shaft. Wolpaka, not knowing any better, tied his axe with
a bark string. He had hardly begun cutting when it snapped. Orei
said, "You had better look in the forest for a new string". Whilst
his friend was in the forest, Orei finished felling. The tree was
very high and began to swing. An ant-nest fell southward, and came
down near the mouth of the Wanggo River. But the nest of a wood-
pigeon was hurled northward and landed near Beow. After some time
his friend returned. Only then did Orei teach him that he should
use rattan for an axe-string. "Dunce", he said, "this will not work.
Turn around; there you will find rattan".*

The tree had fallen across the Yób River, and Orei told Wolpaka:
"You belong here. It is your home. Go up the river." And he presented him with the *yevale* of the yam, of the *tuba* (Indonesian for
fish-poison) and of the stone axe, who were all with him in the
canoe. And Wolpaka set out. He accidentally lost his penis shell.
It changed into a turtle which crawled into the river. When Wolpaka
became aware of the loss, he put all his things down and went in
search. He found the shell and tried to pick it up. But the shell
said: "No; I am a turtle now, and I want to stay here". Wolpaka
returned to the spot where he had left his possessions, meaning to

---

*   In Kwél the story of Orei and Wolpaka is related as one of the
    adventures of Nak and Telle, a context which seems more appro-
    priate.

pick them up. But his things cried out: "No, no! Leave us here, because this is henceforward our country." Thus Wolpaka continued, until he arrived at the head of the river, where he remained.

But Orei had continued on his way in his canoe, putting *yevale* ashore everywhere. Arriving at the Omboge, he set down Daberow and Alabel. Daberow changed into a cassowary, Alabel into an eel. At the mouth of the Watseda, Yegerep went ashore, and near the Ugu, Sangwol. At Bádgóbberter, in the vicinity of Kekayu, he set down Bád, who entered a large rock which is still there. At Grigripelebák he put a young girl ashore. By now the canoe had become very light, and therefore he no longer let anyone out. All that had been left in his canoe were the trees, the mud and the water-lilies. He rowed straight on to the head of the river. There, at Mallin, he put down his punting-pole. It changed into a bamboo clump. The canoe had run aground. To set it afloat again, he went down on his knees. The imprint of his knees is still visible there. But he did not get the canoe afloat. He now unloaded everything that was left: all the various kinds of sago, the yellow clay, the shells, the frogs, the thick bamboo (Indonesian: *buluh*) and the *abal* (a thorny kind of wood), and also a young girl whom he had brought with him. Orei stayed there together with her. And he left the canoe where it was. It had delivered all the *yevale* on its way, each with his own *arow* and his own country.

My informants of Polka (Kekayu) admit that they certainly did not mention the names of all the *yevale* who were put ashore from the *orei*-canoe, but they are absolutely positive in their assertion that *all* the *yevale* came by the *orei*-canoe. Those of the other rivers [note that the journey here described is confined to the Obat River only!] also came to their country by the *orei*-canoe. Some assume that the canoe, at high water, travelled overland to the Maro River, something which is technically quite feasible. Others believe that Orei went all the way up the Maro River first, and then returned to follow the Obat. The main point is that all *yevale* originated from the *orei*-tree, that they were brought to their home country in the *orei*-canoe, and that they all carried a *kupör* with them as the symbol of their authority.

Editor's comment. Before turning to Verschueren's exposition on the nature and functions of the *yevale* (and to his theories on that subject) in the next section we will need to dwell for a while on the factual content of the above myth, in particular the identification of the *yevale* with the *orei*-tree and their close association with the *kupör*. In ms. A Verschueren makes a few revealing comments on this point, but before examining them one purely formal problem will have to be solved. This is the regular recurrence in mss B and A of an alternative term for *kupör*, namely *kupoi*, or, less frequently, *kupoï*. The documents being typewritten copies of Verschueren's handwritten papers, it is obvious that the copyist (Father Hoeboer) had difficulties with Verschueren's handwriting. As it is highly improbable for *kupoi* to become corrupted into something like *kupör* in swift writing, whereas it is easily conceivable that *kupör* would be read as *kupoi* or *kupoï*, I have accepted *kupör* as the correct term.

In ms. A Verschueren states that *orei* is the special kind of wood of which bullroarers are made everywhere in South New Guinea. "The Marind name is *gonggei*." From Van Baal 1966 we learn that the word *gonggei* (*gongai*) is also used as an alternative term for bullroarer (*sosom*) and even for *pahui*. The point is of interest because in this same ms. A, Verschueren repeatedly designates the concept of *kupör* with the word *orei*. Apparently, the two terms are interchangeable. But there is more to it than that. *Orei* refers not only to the bullroarer or bullroarer-like object used in ritual, and not only to the tree, either, but also to Orei, the leader of all the *yevale* taken by him to their respective territories in a canoe which again is called *orei*. It is reminiscent of the fact that the Marind-anim bullroarer, *sosom*, is in effect the same as Sosom, the *dema*, who is the brother of *Waba*, the central *dema* of the great Mayo ritual.

Nevertheless, there is also a difference. Among the Marind the *sosom* (bullroarer) is terminologically differentiated from the *tang*, the bullroarer-like object used in all magic, the object, too, which is presented to all the new initiates at the conclusion of the Mayo initiation (Van Baal 1966:534). Outwardly, *tang* and *sosom* differ only in as far as the one has a hole for a cord to swing the implement by, and the other does not. Among the Yéi the two are terminologically identical as well. There, too, the new initiate receives one (a *kupör*) during his initiation. Whether this is one with or without a hole will be left undecided; really important only is the fact that it is handed out to young males at their initiation, and that every male must become identical with *orei* by symbolically swallowing the implement. The ideal is to become an *orei-kerau*, that is, an *orei*-man or medicine-man (cf. Chapter V). What, then, does the implement stand for?

There can be no doubt on this point. As early as 1963 I argued that everywhere in South New Guinea and Australia the bullroarer is the symbol par excellence of the male sex. Three years later I elaborated the point with regard to the bullroarer among the Marind-anim (Van Baal 1966:485ff.) and demonstrated that the *pahui* is identical with the bullroarer, and, like the Yéi-nan *pöggul*, symbolizes a large penis piercing a small vulva (Van Baal 1966:724-43). This symbolism of the *kupör* turns the myth of the *orei*-tree from just another myth of origin than that of Ndiwe, into its logical as well as symbolical complement. Ndiwe's men brought female symbols to the territory, the *kupe* which are kept in the centres (navels) of their respective territories. In contrast, Orei's men brought male symbols, *kupör*, which as such stand for the shafts which turn the *kupe* from mere stones into formidable war-clubs or ceremonial *pöggul*. We noted above (Section 2) that on the site of a *komen* hardwood poles are never absent, and also that, on the return of a war party, the *gab-elul* leaves the remains of his *pöggul* (notably its shaft) at the residence of the *arow yevale*, a residence described in the same terms as that of a *komen*. One thing is certain: the *komen* (*kupe*) is by origin associated with warfare, which kind of association is not foreign to the *kupör*, either, for when the central headhunting pole of a new house is erected, a *kupör* is planted at its side (see Chapter VII, Section 3).

We will have to go more deeply into this matter. To that end a closer examination of all Verschueren's data and theories on the *yevale* is necessary. Not only are his explanations often confusing, but his facts also give rise to controversy. For instance, he states that all the *yevale* originate from the *orei*-tree and that they all brought a *kupör* with them. Yet there are also female *yevale*, amd though we are not told anywhere that they, too, brought a *kupör*, this is nowhere denied, either.

5. *The yevale and their role in the headhunting ritual*

At the outset of his observations on the *yevale* in the uncompleted chapter on Religion and Magic in ms. B, Verschueren states that the term *yevale* is best translated with "spirit", more or less in the sense of the Marindinese term *dema*, but with the exclusion of the latter's connotation of totem-ancestor. The *yevale* constitute a group of anthropomorphic beings, gifted with exceptional powers, who are spread all over the territory. After performing their extraordinary feats, they all settled in one or another area inside the country, always the basin (*arow*) of one of the numerous affluents of the Maro River, where they retired in some such place as a tree, a well, a brook or a stone. Obviously, the tree or the stone is not considered as a *yevale* by the Yéi, being no more than the place of residence of a definitely man-like being. Such places are revered as sacred places by all the people of the relevant *arow*.

There are male and female *yevale*, and though apparently the Telle preferably worship female and the Nak male *yevale*, this cannot be generalized for the whole of the territory. In ms. A, however, the author is more specific, saying:

Among the *yevale* males and females are of about equal numbers. It is intriguing that almost all the female *yevale* are found in Telle territory, and the male ones in that of Nak. This once again stresses the male-female relation, and this time not only in the social field, but in the magico-religious one as well.

Editor's comment. Actually, this paragraph contains one of the most dubious of all of Verschueren's statements concerning the *yevale*. The myth related in the previous section rarely ever mentions the sex of the *yevale* who were put down from the *orei*-canoe, though the story seems to imply that, with two exceptions, they all were males. Of these two exceptions one is the consort of Orei, the other a girl disembarked somewhere near the head of the river; moreover, neither of the two is explicitly connected with a specific *arow*. The one *yevale* who, besides Orei, is explicitly identified as a man is Wolpake. He is the *arow-yevale* of the Yób River, which is not a Nak but a Telle *arow* (cf. the map in Section 3 of Chapter II). What is more, the final phrase of the quotation from ms. A with its emphasis on Nak and Telle and their male-female relation strongly supports the suspicion that the association of the sex of the *yevale* with that of Nak or

Telle is a generalization based on an over-simplified interpretation of the existing moiety-dualism rather than on the facts yielded by research. Verschueren's interpretation of the impact of moiety dualism represents, in fact, a misjudgement of the dialectics inherent in dualism. It never goes to the extent of opposing an all-male to an all-female moiety. Besides, the myth itself repeatedly presents Telle as a male.

The *worship* of the *yevale* is connected primarily with the fact that they unite the various *jéi* occupying a common *arow* through a new bond of a religious nature. They all share the same *yevale*.

What, then, is the relation between the *yevale* and humans? The *yevale* are *not* creators; hardly any of them are said to have made or transformed anything at all. They are not spirits of the dead or ancestors, either, because they have acquired their functions in their human, corporeal form, a form cast off by the dead.[5] What they really are is guardians of the rules of morality, judges of the good and evil acts of mankind. Virtually all of them are associated with one or other aspect of human life, with regard to which specific aspect they give the individual their support or punish him when he misbehaves. Because of the strong impact of war on Yéi-nan culture, several of them have a close relation with headhunting.

Editor's comment. Ms. A is more detailed on one point. It says that some things which are dear to the Yéi originated or received their present form through the medium of *yevale*, adding that we never find this stressed in the mythology, and thus conveniently forgetting that the myth of the *orei*-tree makes mention of several of such cases. One page earlier the same document states that admittedly several *yevale* had all sorts of goods which are useful for mankind, such as yams and fish, with them on their arrival in their specific *arow*, but also that no indications are found of any specific relation between a *yevale* and his treasures, or the descent or family relations of the *jéi* concerned. In other words, there is no totem relation. Ms. B advances similar views. It states that in a few, rather rare, cases the *yevale* appear as a kind of totem-ancestor, but adds that, nevertheless, these totems have no specific relationship with the peple concerned. The author stresses that this totemic element is found only among the southern Yéi, and that this suggests borrowing from neighbours, notably the Marind, based on a partial or complete misunderstanding.

In the introduction to the present chapter the remark was made that the totemism of the Yéi, far from having been adopted from the Marind, is akin to that of the more easterly tribes, a view which was corroborated in my comment on Nak and Telle (Section 3, above). The myth of the *orei*-tree includes several examples of a *yevale* turning into an animal (fish, an echidna, a cassowary), and even speaks of the *yevale* of the yam and the *tuba*. As the *yevale* concerned are bound to a specific *arow*, and every *arow* has connections with at least one *jéi*, a relation between *yevale*, totem and *jéi* seems obvious. But Verschueren denies this, at least for the more northerly communities. He also denies the existence of totemic food taboos. Now, totemism can exist without

food taboos but not without clans or other social groupings with
an exclusive relation with the totem. Must we agree with Verschueren, then, that totemism is, at the very best, an imported institution among the Yéi? Most certainly not. Later, in the chapter
on Death and Burial, we will come across the use of a *maker*, a
sign used for identifying either its manufacturer or a particular
addressee. These *maker* are of a totemic nature and are used as the
distinctive mark of the totem group concerned, a fact which is
documented in detail by Nevermann. In other words, totems *are*
connected with groups, and there are no indications that this is
confined to the southern groups.

On the contrary, the data collected by Wirz provide undeniable
evidence that the more northerly *jéi*, too, had their totems. Perhaps not all of them did, for Wirz states (1925(III):202) that
the Yéi include clans without a totem, a circumstance due to the
fact that their *yevale* (translated as "ancestor" in the sense of
clan-ancestor by him) had no relation with a particular natural
species or object. In this translation of *yevale* with "ancestor"
lies the reason for Verschueren's stubborn refusal to recognize
the totemism of the Yéi as genuine. He does not deny that certain
jéi have specific relations with certain *yevale* and consider these
yevale as belonging to them, but only that these relations can be
described in terms of descent. His point is that *yevale* are *not*
ancestors, even though in some cases they do resemble them. For
Verschueren, who derived his knowledge of totemism from the Marind-
anim form, the descent relation is essential for totemism. This
explains his contempt for Wirz and Nevermann, as well as his attempts to play down the facts concerning Yéi-nan totemism to the
extent of making himself guilty of tendentious description.

The *yevale* punish those who misbehave, for which the sanctions
applied are illness and death. The punishing aspect is predomi-
nant and is more in evidence than those of mutual support and
assistance. In the chapter on Sickness and Healing quite a number
of data have been assembled which are unanimous on the point that
the cause of illness lies invariably in sins against tribal rules
and norms. These illnesses are of two kinds, namely male or female, and it is interesting that the male illnesses are, in principle, always curable, whereas the female ones, those caused by
the female *yevale* Baderam, may bring on death. But we should not
anticipate too much what will be discussed in detail in Chapter VI, and confine ourselves to a consideration of what ms. B
has to say on the nature of the *yevale* in general. This is that,
all things considered, the *yevale* are not feared because they
are respected, but respected because they are feared, an idea
subscribed to also in ms. A.

This statement is too general, however. Ms. A, without for a
moment denying the fear inspired by the *yevale*, stresses that
they also give help. Every *yevale* has his own *arow* and inside
that *arow* takes care of everything, though this care may often
be specialized. One will ensure a good game-bag, another a rich
catch of fish; one will provide fire, another garden produce. But
in principle they are all universal in their responsibility,
which is most emphatically reflected in the expectation that the

yevale will give assistance on headhunting expeditions. In the
sphere of headhunting the active communication of the local community with its *yevale* is at its most intensive. After every
headhunt the heads taken are immediately taken to the *yevale*'s
residence to show him the catch. And that is not all. A grand
feast is held in the presence of the heads in the same spot. The
area around the *yevale*'s residence is cleaned up and decorated,
and the ceremony is concluded with a meal. Besides, even before
the expedition the community of the males has visited the *yevale*
to invoke his protection, because, according to the senior men,
formerly the *yevale* went with the headhunters in person to see
to it that they made a good catch. Ms. B discusses these topics
in more general terms. It states that the abodes of the *yevale*
were kept meticulously clean, that their assistance was invoked
whenever the people concerned were in need of anything, and that
it was more specifically a headhunt which prompted them to sol-
icit the *yevale*'s assistance and to offer a thanksgiving when
all had gone well.

    After a short observation on the respect paid the *yevale* also
when the Yéi speak of them in daily life, the document turns to
a more theoretical consideration of the subject.

Characteristic of the *yevale* is their magical power, their underworld aspect: they are said to originate from the *orei*-tree (a magic
palm); they travelled in an *orei*-canoe; they all brought a chip of
the *orei*-tree with them as a magic implement (the *kupör* or bullroarer), and they finally disappeared into the ground. The latter
circumstance contrasts them with the sun. As for the sun, the few
times there seems to be mention of an absolute, supreme being, this
being is the sun. Finally, some details from the total cycle of
myths give rise to the thesis that they all form part of a single
great moon-myth, the moon as such standing in opposition to the sun.

6. Editor's synthesis

    The author's final observations on magic and the underworld, on
the possible role of the sun as a supreme being, and on the relation between the *yevale* and a supposed moon-myth tell us more
about the difficulties of the author in placing the *yevale* in a
more general context than about the forms of belief current among
the Yéi-nan. The available data do not give any ground for such
speculations. There is never any mention of an underworld, nor
is there any mythical material on hand which can be interpreted
as a moon-myth, let alone that the moon is mentioned in it. References to the sun are confined to the statement that the souls of
men who have died in combat go skyward in the direction of the
sun (see Chapter VII, Section 1), and nowhere is there any question
of a supreme being. The one thing that is certain is that the
author uses the latter term loosely, even extremely loosely. In
one place (p. 5) he refers to the *yevale* as supreme beings!

    Besides, these reflections on the nature of the *yevale* general-
ly are always *ad hoc* and dependent on a fortuitous context which
at the given moment was foremost in the author's mind. A case in

point is the statement about the respect always shown the *yevale*.
This is not true. They are regularly chased away without any sign
of respect (Chapter III, Section 3; Chapter VIII, Sections 1, 2).
Another is the statement that *all the yevale* came by the *orei*-
canoe and carried a *kupör*. I have already expressed my doubts
on this point. It is evident that the *yevale* are of different
kinds, and above all we are in need of a more systematic description of these various kinds.

There must be myriads of *yevale*. We are told that they sneak
unseen into the communal house and make the children ill (Chapter III, Section 3). Before hauling a newly hewn dug-out from its
place in the jungle, the *yevale* must be chased away (Chapter VIII,
Section 1); the same must be done at the pigsties before a pig-
feast. Apparently these *yevale* are just malignant. A really malignant one is the ogress of Chapter IX, Section 2, who is killed by
crocodiles or annihilated by fire. In all these cases there is
no ancestorship involved at all; they are merely (more or less)
localized dangerous spirits who have to be avoided, chased away
or, in myth, killed. Even the benign woman *yevale* of Chapter IX,
Section 1, cannot be an ancestress, either; she is carried off by
the Boadzi. There is no reference to the *orei*-tree in connection
with the *yevale* mentioned thus far. Apparently informants have
not been questioned on this point.

If they had been, the result might still have been negative because the *yevale* originating from the *orei*-tree are different.
They are associated with authority over the *arow* of their area
of residence, with the origin of certain plants and animals, and
with the headhunting ritual, in other words, with positive functions of protection for certain specified processes and activities, among them hunting, fishing, gardening, the fire, and, the
most important of all, headhunting (see above). Not mentioned above
are the *yevale* involved in healing rituals. They are, for the so-
called "male" illnesses, the bamboo and the rattan *yevale*. No
names are mentioned for them, but their totemic relation with
plants which provide the raw materials for the implements of the
headhunter (the bamboo knife and the handle of the club respectively) makes this understandable. The situation is different with
respect to Baderam (Chapter III, Section 3; Chapter VI), the
yevale of the female illnesses who spirits a woman's apron into
her victim's body. Reportedly a special myth is told about her.
We are kept in ignorance of its contents, but a woman's apron is
not quite congruous with a *kupör*, an instrument, moreover, which
is more beneficial in its effects.

The ancestor role imputed to the *yevale* by Wirz has already
been discussed (Section 5 above), our conclusion being that the
relationship between a *yevale* and "his" *jéi* is not definable in
terms of descent but in the vaguer ones of "belonging to". We
will not need to return to this point, as we will to that of the
kupör. Of some four or five of the *yevale* it is explicitly stated
that they had their *kupör* with them, and of one of these that
Orei handed him his *kupör* at his departure in token of his authority. The supposition that the term *kupör* is used here as an alternative for *pöggul*, the ritual implement which is the symbol of

the *gab-elul*'s office (Chapter II, Section 2), is not too far-
fetched. It certainly argues in favour of an *arow yevale* whose
special function is the protection of the party of headhunters, whom he accompanies on their expedition. The fact that
the *kupör* (whether or not it is a *pöggul*) functions as a symbol
of authority constitutes another argument against the supposition
that female *yevale* could ever have carried one.

However, a caution is well in place here. Although the various
yevale all acquired their own *arow* in the course of their journey
in the *orei*-canoe, this does not mean that they are all *arow*
yevale. The *arow yevale* is the spirit of the headhunting ritual
who affiliates several *jéi* into a common worship as well as headhunting unit (Chapter II, Section 2; Section 5 above). On p. 51
Verschueren also stated that not all *yevale*, but only several of
them are connected with headhunting. Yet, *yevale* not associated
with headhunting have their own *arow* as well. The point is that
the term *arow* denotes not a genealogical, but a geographical concept (Chapter II, Section 1) and can be used in different con-
texts. If one tries to trace the *orei*-canoe journey down the Obat
River on the map, one glance will suffice to convince the student
that it stopped at many more rivers which became the specific
arow of the *yevale* who disembarked there than there are or pos-
sibly can be headhunting-*arow*. The *arow yevale*, or war-gods, form
a special group among the numerous *yevale* who maintain positive
relations with certain *jéi*. As war-gods, they are more appropriate bearers of the *kupör* than anyone. Though other male *yevale*
may also be associated with the *kupör* as the indispensable implement in most forms of magic, the *kupör* is closely connected with
the headhunting pole in the centre of the communal house (Section
4, p. 49), and, as we have just noted, may also be associated with
the *pöggul*.

7. *A note on headhunting*

Headhunting was instituted by Ndiwe. Though headhunting as such
is not explicitly mentioned in the story, the fact that Ndiwe
equipped his men with *kupe*, the essential component of the headhunter's club, and moreover two of them with a *pöggul*, leaves no
room for doubt on this point. The war-gods proper, however, are
the *yevale* originating from Orei. This circumstance alone is
enough for us to assume some kind of a relationship between the
myth of Ndiwe and that of Orei. Verschueren, too, inclined toward
this view, but his reflections on this point led him into speculations of a pseudo-historical nature which are not very helpful.
In a note on the Orei myth he wrote:

The contrast between the social cycle dealing with the origin of
mankind and that concerning the *yevale* is evident. Both cycles run
parallel to the extent that neither the origin of mankind nor that
of the *yevale* is considered as a tribal affair, but both are put in
a kind of "international" context. Ndiwe accompanied not only the
Yéi, but also the upper Bian people, the Boadzi and the Kanum on
their path through life. The *yevale* who congregated in the *orei-*

tree belonged to the Boadzi, the Marind and the Yéi. But there is
also a contrast between mankind and the *yevale*. Mankind came into
existence earlier, and the *yevale* owe their origin to human beings
(the Kanum) who were already present. The activities of the *yevale*
are of no importance for mankind until well after they have been
released through human interference.

Editor's comment. I do not believe that this brings us to the
heart of the matter. In order to arrive at a more meaningful interpretation we should first summarize what we know of the headhunting practices of the Yéi. Our information on this point is
scant.

In the introduction to the myth of Ndiwe, I pointed out (Section 1 above) that the Yéi are unique in their treatment of their
war booty. The heads were suspended from a two-metre long rattan
loop, with the long bones of the victims fastened at either end
to each side of the loop, like the rungs of a ladder (cf. **Wirz**
1925(III):Tafel VIII no. 1, and cover). The artefact was ultimately suspended from the central pole of the house, where it marked the dividing-line between the *soama* and *wake*. The presence of
the long bones (those of the legs and arms of the victims) is
suggestive of cannibalism. The latter supposition is confirmed
in one of the teachers' papers and in the myth of Wane, the good
sister, at the end of Chapter IX, Section 1, where cannibalism
is presented as a normal practice.

We also know that of the *gab-elul* of a particular *arow* the first
in rank was the headman whose *jéi* "owned" the *arow yevale* (Chapter II, Section 2). And further that, in spite of Verschueren's
eulogies on the *gab-elul* as an arbiter and whatever else (Chapter II, Section 2), he was first and foremost a (ritual) war-
leader (Chapter VIII, Section 4). Of his functions as such we
only know that, before a war party set out, the community of the
males paid its respects to the *arow yevale* and invoked his protection, and above all requested his participation in the expedition (Section 5 above). Once the party had met the enemy, the
headman tried to thrust his *pöggul* between the legs of a fleeing
enemy so that its fretwork top broke off. He would then raise the
shaft of the implement, now simply a club with a *kupe* at its end,
and fell the enemy by striking him between the shoulder-blades.
The club was taken back home together with the remains of the
shattered fretwork, which had been collected on the spot, and
were afterwards deposited near the residence of the *arow yevale*
(cf. ms. B, p. 31). The document does not tell what happened following the felling of the victim, but on this point we can be
certain. As everywhere in these parts, the victim will have been
beheaded with the aid of a bamboo knife. The document restricts
itself to the information that on its return, the war party goes
to the residence of the *arow yevale* for a thanksgiving. The *gab-
elul*, after taking the stone ring (*kupe*) off the shaft of his
damaged *pöggul*, carries it ceremonially around the *misár*, the
pole with the heads, and inserts the shaft in the ground near
the *yevale*.

Ms. A gives additional information (on p. 14). The heads are

taken to the *yevale*'s place for display (apparently they are suspended from the *misár*). The place is cleaned and decorated, and
the ceremony is concluded with a meal. The author does not provide any further information, but there can hardly be any doubt
that this was a cannibalistic meal.

One problem that remains is where the *yevale*'s residence was.
Obviously this was at the *komen*. In Section 2 above we pointed
out that the *komen* is quite often chosen as a place of residence
by a *yevale*. The description of the place testifies that it is
suitable for the holding of a headhunting ceremony. It is decorated with croton shrubs and hardwood poles. The latter feature
in particular suggests that the place was once used for some ceremonial purpose including the planting of hardwood poles. The
only occasion about which we know of such a thing happening is
the final headhunting ritual (particularly in connection with the
misár and the shaft of the *gab-elul*'s *pöggul*). Besides, as has
been argued in Section 4 above, the *komen is*, ritually, a *kupe*,
and as such is directly associated with headhunting. On top of
all this, what the *gab-elul* does on the return of the war party,
namely remove the *kupe* from the shaft of his damaged *pöggul* which
he then inserts in the ground near the *yevale*, is the exact complement of what the ancestors did on their return from the campaign against the foreign occupants of the country. They removed
their *kupe* and laid them down in the centre of their respective
territories as the latter's navels.

The symbolism is plain. Ndiwe was accompanied by his mother,
Atu, the Bad Woman of Boadzi ritual and mythology (Section 2
above). She is the instigator of the practice of headhunting and
is identical with the *kupe*, the implement which the ancestors
placed on the ground as a vulva awaiting renewed copulation with
the *kupör* (*pöggul*). In my analysis of the functions of the *pahui*,
the Marind-anim *pöggul*, I arrived at the conclusion that headhunting is in these parts a symbolic form of copulation (Van
Baal 1966:725-45). It may in fact even be classified as a fertility rite, which conclusion I elaborated in my contribution to
Gilbert H. Herdt's book on ritual homosexuality in Melanesia (in
the press). Fertility is, ultimately, the prerogative of the
males, and they promote it by killing: life springs from death,
just as it does from sexual intercourse. The interconnection of
the two is embodied in the *pöggul*, the death-inflicting implement
which is at the same time a penis piercing a vulva.

Subconsciously, the men are aware that their almost exclusive
claims to fertility are void. In this context Verschueren's remarks on the temporal precedence of Ndiwe over the *yevale* are of
interest. Only, it is not mankind in general, nor even Ndiwe who
came prior to the *yevale*, but who came first of all is Atu, the
great mother of both Ndiwe and mankind, who lies waiting as a
stone vulva - also a deadly implement - for renewed fertilization
by the warriors, the *orei*-men, the bearers of *kupör* and *pöggul*,
who, like the *yevale*, are maleness incarnate. Yet no mention is
made of the *komen*. On the surface, all the honour goes to the
males. All the same, the presence of the woman, whether she be
called Atu, *kupe* or *komen*, is the basic condition for the honour

that is paid to the *arow yevale*. And it is probably no coincidence that Orei and Ndiwe both came from the east. The east is
the direction in which most of the Yéi-nan's headhunting expeditions led them.

To a reader unacquainted with the ethnography of the southern
New Guinea lowlands, these comments must seem a mystification
rather than an explanation. However, if he perseveres, he may
learn in the next chapter how deeply the ideology of the *kupōr*
and of ideal maleness has affected the ways and thoughts of the
Yéi-nan.

Chapter V

Initiation

Initiation begins when a girl has her first menses. The girl must
stay in her place in the *wake* for about a month. She is not allowed to stir from it. Meat and fish are forbidden. A younger girl is
commissioned to keep her company and to bring her all the things
she needs. She will also, whenever necessary, empty the *bogguteo*
(basket of plaited sago-leaves) which the menstruating girl has
been given to put her left-overs and other refuse in. [Nothing is
said about how the girl relieves herself; she will probably go outside to do this, under the supervision of some older woman.]
 Not long after the beginning of her seclusion, the men of the
house retire into the forest to celebrate the *orei*-ritual. This is
also called *köllu-köllu* and forms part of the boys' initiation.
When this ritual approaches its final phase, the girl is taken by
her parents into the bush, where a crude hut has been constructed
at some distance from the *wake* by inserting palm-leaves in the
ground in a circle and plaiting the leaves together into a kind of
beehive. The hut resembles that which bird-hunters construct near
a well as a hide-out from which to spy on their prey. In this hut
the girl installs herself with her mother to await the final ritual.
In the afternoon the men come out of the forest. When near the hut,
they start singing the *köllu*. After "swallowing" their *kupör*, they
conjure them up again from their bodies, covered with blood, which
is sprinkled over the hut. After dancing a few times around the
hut, the men finally retire to the *soama*. By then it is already
pitch-dark, and mother and daughter remain in the hut. Early the
next morning the mother takes her daughter to a nearby brook for
a bath, something the girl has not enjoyed since the onset of her
menstruation. She then receives the *gend sinak*, the long, red
painted apron (hanging down to the ground) which will be her daily
attire until she marries. In addition, she is adorned with bird of
paradise feathers, croton twigs are slipped into her armlets, and
her face [and body?] is painted red. Then she is led back to the
wake with some solemnity. She is now a *boatsyap*, and may no longer
enter the *soama*, and in any case has to avoid the company of males.
According to rumours, formerly the *boatsyap* had to pass the day in
a special girls' house, where they were supervised by older women,
in the same way as the boys in the *korár bö* were supervised by
older men. The suggestion that the girls' house might be used for
homosexual purposes was firmly rejected.

At the moment when, in the *wake*, a girl's first menstruation begins,
any boys of roughly the same age are similarly secluded in the
soama. They are forbidden to enter the *wake* any longer, and are
subjected to similar food taboos as the girl. Once the girl has

retired to the hut for the final ceremony, the fathers of these
boys will take them to the river for a bath. Back in the *soama*,
the boys are painted black but receive no pubic cover. From now on
they are *kudjer-por*, charcoal or black boys, and have to avoid all
contact with, and even the proximity of, women and girls. They may
not stay in the *soama* during the day. Their home then is the *korár
bö*.[1]

Early each morning, at the call of a certain bird (the *töbtu*),
the headman rouses the boys with the call: "Arise, the snakes are
still coiled up and might awaken", a phrase which actually refers
to the women. The boys take fire from the *soama* to kindle the *korár
ben*, "the fire of the place". It is always in a spot some 50 metres
from the *soama*, preferably one which offers a wide view of the land-
scape. This fire-making is their first job. There is nothing sacral
or religious about it, but it is just for common use. In the early
morning chilliness it is a good place to gather at.

On his entry into the *korár bö*, the boy is entrusted to the care
of a mentor, one of the men of the *soama*, either a married one or
a *wapo tíntyau*, a fully initiated young man. In addition to being
his supervisor, he is also the boy's pederast. He is never a close
relative, such as a father, brother, or father's brother. But he
is certainly not a mother's brother as among the Marind, which, in
view of the pattern of settlement of the Yéi, is an obvious impossibility. Homosexual intercourse with the boy (in this area always
anal) is neither a reward to the mentor for his guardianship, nor
an exclusive prerogative of his. When the *kudyer-por* commit sodomy
among themselves, no one objects, as they would do if they did so
with a younger boy who has not yet been admitted to the *korár bö*.
Sodomy is the mentor's duty; it is his task to see to the boy's
masculinization. Coming straight from the *soama*, where he has been
secluded like a girl, the boy is still girlish, and sodomy is the
main means of making him strong and masculine and a good warrior.

The boy's life in the community of the *korár ben* is geared to
that objective. The techniques of warfare, including those of evad-
ing flying arrows and fending off blows, are taught and exercised
here. His mentor is not the boy's only instructor. He has regular
contacts with all the older men, who enjoy telling the boys of
their own adventures and heroic exploits. They are also schooled in
tribal lore and customs here, and the whole period in the *korár bö*
can in fact be considered as one of purposive education.

The first initiation of the boys follows later, namely when another girl in the *wake* of the settlement has her first menstruation.
They are secluded [where?] and subjected to a strict fast. After
three or four weeks the *gab-elul* calls the novices to the bush, to
a place not far from the hut for the girl who has had her first
menses. The boys have to line up, and the *gab-elul* with a few older
men stand facing them. They cast a charm on their *kupör* (bullroarers), which during the previous days have been busily swung around
and manipulated. Usually the *kupör* will have been rubbed with
kunai-grass and lime, a treatment promoting the production of a
high-pitched squeaking noise. Now the boys have to open their
mouths, with the tongue lifted upwards. They are told that the
kupör will enter their bodies under the tongue. After the uttering

of some formulas by the senior men, the kupör suddenly appear to
have vanished, and the boys have to dance, i.e. leap up with both
feet off the ground. Suddenly the older men step forward and pull
the kupör out of the boys' bodies. If it comes out of a leg, thigh,
arm or foot, then the boy will become a good orei-por, or orei-man.
If it appears from the vicinity of the genitals, this is a hint
that the boy is a potential sorcerer, who in time may be sent to
the Kanum to receive a training in black magic, something which cannot be obtained within the boundaries of the Yéi-nan tribe.[2] Finally, the boys who have passed the test successfully[3] receive a new
kupör from their mentors. They must treat it with the utmost reverence. The old men say that initially the orei [i.e. the kupör] in
the hands of the boys is like an infant which needs extreme care
in order to become strong and vigorous in the boys.

Boys who have received theur orei will go to the big forest on
a day that is not further specified, to some equally unspecified
place, far away from every settlement or pathway, to plant a misár,
or hardwood stick. After their return, they never go back to look
at the misár. Only a man who feels he is growing old and is approaching death will go back to the place where he has planted the
stick and pull it out of the ground where he once inserted it.[4]

The second initiation ritual, probably the tribal ritual proper,
is that which takes place when the male community congregates near
the menstruation hut. Some weeks before, the men assemble in deep
secrecy far away in the great forest. Women are not allowed to see
them at all. Here the men spend some weeks in seclusion. They sub-
mit to a severe fast. The first four days they are not even allowed to drink water. They consume various magical herbs known only
to the older men, one after another, beginning with sago-gum [what-
ever that may be], and changing later to leaves and bark. They sing
and swing the bullroarers. All sexual intercourse is strictly forbidden. If the men had intercourse, the orei would not be able to
slip easily into the body, but would become stuck somewhere and
kill its owner, it is said.

From the stories I gather that the men gradually work themselves
up into a trance. Finally, those who are fully possessed by Orei
and have become one with him congregate at a distance of some twenty
or more metres from the menstruation hut (where the girl has just
entered). At this spot the men have constructed a kind of arch, on
which the trance-struck men hang their kupör. Under the arch, placed
in the earth, are a number of kava cups, one for each of the participants. The young men chew kava, which is spat into the cups, to
which the performing men add herbs, such as wild ginger, burnt
young sago-leaves, and nellidya (the bark of a tree). After taking
a little food [and, of course, the kava, but this is not mentioned
in the text], the men stand up, take their kupör from the arch, and
form into a line. Now they all strike up the köllu-köllu song. The
performers, stirring up their spirits by leaping and shouting, swallow their kupör (under the tongue, as usual). The swallowing of the
kupör must, of course, be understood in a magical sense. Actually,
the kupör disappears under the armpit, whence it emerges again at
its "reappearance". The insertion of the implement under the tongue
probably has a sexual connotation. However that may be, the men

proceed jumping and singing to the hut in which the girl sits with
her mother. Some of the words of the song are as follows:

> *Udöp oh, Bomön eh, na kwa riba oh ah oh*
> *Nobo no ah, Keinang eh, na oh ah eh....*
> Udöp, Bomön
> Give me light, make it clear to me, Nobo, Keinang,
> Come, come to me ...[5]

When the performers have arrived at the hut, they suddenly re-pro-
duce their *kupör* from their bodies, but now the implements are
covered with blood. Blood also gushes from their mouth and nose.
They sprinkle the blood of the *kupör* over the hut as they dance
around it. The dancing becomes ever livelier, and they go round
several times. The singing becomes more and more excited, the dancing and leaping wilder and wilder. This goes on until long after
darkness has fallen. Then they silently retire to the *soama*.

My enquiries about the meaning of these rites were countered with
the statement that the men must become one with Orei. They must become *orei kerau*, men who are *orei*, in contradistinction to *orei ene
kerau*, men who are of [belong to?] *orei* [or Orei?]. Their unifica-
tion with Orei renders the men strong and healthy. Men who have
thus acquired the power of Orei as part of themselves have the power
- each in accordance with his own *yevale*[6] - to cure their sick
tribal fellows. When asked why the performance of the rites must
coincide with a young woman's first menstruation, they replied that
it is only when the blood of a virgin flows for the first time that
the *kupör* (that is Orei)[7] is able to glide smoothly into the body
of an *orei*-man. The girl is not allowed to have had sexual intercourse prior to this, as this might enrage Orei, who might strike
the *orei*-man with sickness. He would then be unable to let his
blood flow with the *kupör*. Sexual intercourse, pregnant women, and
dead people must be strictly avoided.

The seclusion of the boys in the *korár bö* ends with the ceremony
of the *possé,* the pubic shell. It takes place at a feast that is an
intercommunal celebration in which groups of both moieties participate. It is preceded by a short period of seclusion of the neophytes, which does not last more than two or three days, and is not
combined with any fasts or taboos. Various neighbouring groups congregate, and they all bring great quantities of arrows. A great
quantity of them is needed because they have to serve as a plat-
form for the boys. The ceremony proper is celebrated in the *soama*
after nightfall. An enormous heap of arrows has been piled up near
the central pole. The men sing *bendol* (a ceremonial song), and the
boys have to stand on the pile one after the other to have their
first pubic shell put on by their mother's brother. The women in
the *wake* can see hardly anything at all of what is going on because
the men crowd around the boys on all sides. The night is passed in
bendol-singing.

Apparently this celebration was not combined with any other ceremonies, unless, by coincidence, a new *gab-elul* had to be inaugur-
ated - an event which will be described in Chapter VIII, Section 3.
The celebration in the *soama* marks the end of the boys' seclusion
as well as of their homosexual relations with their respective men-

tors, They now are *wapo tintyau*, fully initiated young men, entitled
to act as mentors and pederasts to young neophytes themselves.

Editor's comment. Verschueren never described the initiation rites
of the Yéi-nan in any detail. Most of the data presented here had
to be taken from ms. A, containing his summary description of the
more significant aspects of the culture. There was no room in it
for details, and consequently many questions arise to which no
answers can be given. Even so, his description uncovers a not inconsiderable number of highly interesting facts, one of which is
that initiation as such is confined to a few events which take
place during a prolonged period of seclusion which in itself has
as aim the masculinization and invigoration of the boys through
recurrent anal intercourse with their mentors.

The initiation proper, i.e. the admission of the neophytes to
a secret ritual, consists in their gradual integration in successive elements of the *köllu-köllu* ritual. For a complete initiation
at least three successive ritual performances are necessary. Of
the first performance the boys do not get to see anything at all.
It is held during their first period of seclusion in the *soama*
prior to their admission to the *korár bö*. The second is combined
with their actual initiation, though it is uncertain whether they
are allowed to witness the complete proceedings. What is important for the neophytes is that they are acquainted with the bullroarer (*kupör*) and are shown how the implement is "swallowed" in
the form of a spatula. The text, locating the scene of this demonstration at some distance from the menstruation hut, suggests
that it coincides with the dance of the trance-struck initiates
in front of and around the hut. However, this is hardly feasible.
The description is one of a rite concerned exclusively with the
neophytes, in which there can be little question of a trance.
The boys receive a *kupör* from their mentors and are told to bestow great care on the implement. It is probable that at this
stage they are taught by their mentors how to handle the implement. Of course, this does not exclude the possibility of their
presence, one or two days later, at the final rite (e.g., for the
purpose of chewing the kava for the *orei*-men), though this is
far from certain. One should also bear in mind the mysterious
rite with the *misár*. Taking all things together, it seems most
probable that some time is needed before they can be considered
sufficiently "mature" to witness a full performance of the *köllu-
köllu* ritual.

The picture of the initiation that is presented here is sketchy.
Yet one thing is certain· the rites performed are not done so
primarily because the boys must be initiated, but because a girl
has menstruated for the first time in her life. The initiatory
aspect of the *köllu-köllu* is a simple consequence of the fact
that the adolescent boys must be prepared for active participation in the affairs of their social group after reaching a more
mature age. The Yéi-nan take ample time over this maturing process. In the first place, a first menstruation is not a frequent
occurrence in a community counting no more than 70 to 100 people
in all. And in the second place, the neophytes' first complete

participation in the rites does not mark the end of their seclusion in the *korár bö*. This purpose is achieved at the holding of
the feast of the *possé*, and it is far from unlikely that the neophytes have in the meantime attended one or two subsequent *köllu-
köllu* performances.

In spite of so many things about which no information is given,
the facts which are communicated are revealing. The men demonstrate their identity with the *orei*-tree and the *kupör* (bullroarer) with spectacular clarity. They are masculinity incarnate.
More revealing still is the occasion which induces them to re-
confirm their virility: that of a girl becoming a woman. Together
with her mother she keeps concealed in a round hut. We do not
know in what position they remain there, but it is almost certain
that to the men outside it is reminiscent of the *gab-elul*'s morn-
ing-call of "coiled snakes". The entire scene is a mirror reflection of that of the returning war-party to the *konan* in order to
insert the shaft of the *pöggul* in the ground there, thus erecting
the symbol of masculinity next to that of femininity. Actually,
the proceedings of the initiation are marked by a plethora of
male symbols. At the final ceremony the new initiates have to
stand upon an enormous pile of arrows. More eloquent still is the
pathetic scene of the *misár*, the hardwood stick, being planted
in a secret place deep in the forest. It is unmistakably a symbol
of life, the individual male's own life.
    Most intriguing of all is the fact that the *kupör*, apart from
being swallowed, must reappear blood-covered, or as it were
bleeding. The act of sprinkling the blood over the hut gives rise
to the suspicion that a symbolic insemination is meant, though
this idea must be rejected because the young woman inside the
hut is not available for sexual intercourse with the actors either
now or later. On the contrary, she is destined to be given away,
to be exported untainted to another group. The presence of the
mother in the hut points in a totally different direction, namely
to that of the mother in the maternity hut after just giving
birth to a child (Chapter III, Section 3). This allusion is confirmed by the men's fast after they have retired to the forest.
The first four days they are not allowed to drink water, just
like the father (and mother) before the dropping off of the umbilical cord of the newly born baby (Chapter III, Section 3).
    Even so, it is more than simply an allusion to the birth of a
new woman. It is, above all, an assertion by the males that a
birth is not an achievement of the mother alone, but of the males
as well. Considering themselves the true agents of procreation,
they underline this by demonstrating that they have the same
power of bleeding as a menstruating woman. The emergence of a
new woman inspires the men to a demonstration of the superiority
of their sex.
    As everywhere in these parts, though the women are the natural
producers of life, as the headhunting men are of death, the men
attempt to reverse these roles by turning the women into symbols
of death (the death-inflicting *kupe* crowning their clubs) and
themselves, as *orei* incarnate, into symbols of life. If the Yéi

are exceptional in this respect, it is only because they go to
the extreme of claiming for themselves the ability to bleed -
the gift which indicates the women's life-giving potentiality.

Verschueren, who firmly believed the sexual morals of the Yéi-
nan to be superior to those of the Marind, never guessed the
meaning of the data he put forward. This is what makes them so
immensely valuable. They are really genuine. If they have been
"coloured" by the observer's own bias or interest - as all observations are - Verschueren's "colouring" of his data was unable
to affect their real meaning, as the facts prove the opposite of
what he tried to demonstrate: the existence of a great difference
between the sexual implications of Yéi-nan and Marind-anim culture. Actually, the cultic phallism of the Yéi is even more pronounced than that of the Marind. There is question of such a
total identification of man with the *kupör* that the initiate is
referred to as an *orei*-man.

On one point there is reason for doubt, however. The technique
of swallowing the *kupör* and reproducing it in a blood-covered
state appears to be sufficiently difficult to justify the surmise
that not everyone masters it. Besides, the performance is often
combined with symptoms of trance and is described as being risky.
No indications are given of how a young man learns this technique,
though it is a fair guess that the periods of seclusion in the
forest which precede *köllu-köllu* performances are pre-eminently
suitable for instruction and practice in this. From this point
of view it seems possible that in the long run every initiate
will acquire the necessary proficiency, and we would be able to
leave it at that if the term *orei*-man were not also the term for
medicine-man. Now medicine-men are always specialists, and the
description of their healing practices in the next chapter does
not give us any reason to believe that the Yéi-nan form an exception. Taking all things together, the supposition obviously suggests itself that the principal actors in the scene around the
menstruation hut are practising medicine-men, who are surrounded
by a crowd of followers made up of either advanced trainees or
simply dancers.

This would imply that the *kupör* is primarily an implement to be
used by a medicine-man, just as happens to be the case among the
Marind-anim. The parallel is the more intriguing because every
new Marind-anim male initiate receives a *tang* (Yéi *kupör*) at the
end of his initiation period in the *mayo-miráv* (Van Baal 1966:
534) in the same way as Yéi males do in the course of their initiation. What the ordinary Marind initiate does with his *tang*
can only be guessed at (Van Baal 1966:868), as our sole information on this point is confined to its use by their medicine-
men, who - again like the Yéi *orei*-men - are experts in the art
of spiriting the implement away (Van Baal 1966:895-903, 906f.,
912f.). Even so, there is one difference: the Yéi neophyte, before receiving one in effigy, first has the *kupör* of an older
initiate spirited into his body in token of his unity with the
orei. The emphasis on the oneness of every initiate with the
kupör and *orei* is much stronger than among the Marind, just like
the phallic symbolism of the Yéi is generally more pronounced.

Chapter VI

Sickness and Healing

Introductory note

The information on sickness and healing presented in Verschueren's papers is limited and almost certainly deficient. The author deals with the subject first in ms. B, where he gives information on four different types of disease. Later he discusses it in ms. A, the paper intended to give a summary outline of Yéi-nan culture and for this reason of a more general nature than B. With respect to sickness and healing Verschueren's generalizations are clearly biased. He was deeply impressed by the way in which, on several occasions, a patient had to make a full confession of certain sins and wrongdoings before the medicine-man could even begin his treatment. This is a feature that is foreign to other Papuan cultures he was familiar with. Combining this feature with the fact that the Yéi ascribe all sicknesses to the *yevale*, he became easily persuaded that the *yevale* are the guardians of a tribal morality that is far superior to that of neighbouring tribes. And when his informants told him that for the purpose of learning black magic young men might be sent to the Kanum (above, p. 61), he ignored the possibility that these informants might just be trying to conceal a vice of their own at the expense of their enemies, and concluded that black magic is essentially alien to Yéi-nan culture and morality and its occasional use here merely another instance of the pernicious influence of, primarily, the Marind. Consequently, sorcery has no place among the causes of illness and death mentioned in Verschueren's papers.

There is reason for serious doubt on this point. The Yéi-nan themselves assert that the techniques of sorcery must be learnt from the Kanum, thereby confirming that sorcery does occur. Besides, the belief in the lethal effects of sorcery is so widespread and so deeply engrained in the thinking and world view of all Papuan tribes, that its absence here would be outright miraculous. Even so, there is the repeatedly made statement that all sickness derives from the *yevale*. Did Verschueren grossly manipulate his data to prove his point? This is not readily acceptable. What is acceptable is that he interpreted them in his own, biased way, in the same way as when he characterized the *yevale* as the custodians of tribal morality. From his own data (cf. Chapter IV, Section 6) we learned that many of them are dangerous, disreputable characters, and if some are better or less malicious than others, and at times even helpful, this does not suffice to characterize the *yevale* as defenders of virtue. More important still, when they wish to punish offenders they do so in a very peculiar way, namely by spiriting certain objects

into their bodies. The medicine-man must extract these to save
his patient's life. In other words, what the *yevale* actually do
when they punish an offender is make him sick through ordinary
black magic. And this raises the question of whether they really
do this on their own initiative, inspired by a moral standard
which, only too often, seems perfectly alien to them, or at the
invitation of someone who bears a grudge against the victim of
their sorcery. An indication which tends to support the latter
supposition is given by the following quotation from ms. B: "The
yevale are severe but just. Anyone falling seriously ill knows
quite well to what cause he owes this ... The *yevale* do not hurt
the wrong person by way of substitute, but always strike at the
real culprit. However, the *yevale* are not omniscient; they do as
their principal, the owner, has told them. Anyone who takes away
anything from a garden commended to the care of a *yevale* will
certainly be struck. Otherwise it *might* pass that mischief is
done without the *yevale* noticing it."
    Though the wording of the passage just quoted is slightly con-
fused, its purport is evident: to protect a garden against theft,
the owner commends its produce to the protection of some *yevale*,
probably one who has his residence nearby. Of course, there is
nothing illegal about invoking supernatural protection over one's
property, but the methods applied by these supernatural agents
are too closely akin to those of the sorcerer for us not to suspect some kind of material connection. The often disreputable
nature of the *yevale* strongly suggests that their help may also
be requested for less honourable purposes than the protection of
property. If this is accepted, then the problem of the absence
of sorcery will be solved. In that case the sorcerer does exactly the same as every magician, namely invoke the help of some
yevale, whether this be for good or for evil purposes. And this,
in turn, explains the highly ambiguous nature of the *yevale*,
whose malice outweighs their occasional beneficence. Bearing this
in mind, let us now turn to the facts, first of all those communicated in ms. B.

The Yéi-nan distinguish between four kinds of illness, namely *gentye, arga seráuw, nakyasub,* and *akone.* Of these, the *gentye* is a
slight indisposition of a transient nature, such as a headache, a
temperature, a stomach-ache, and so on. It is something the same
as a cold, which should not be given too much attention, though at
times certain herbs (*atsye por*) may have a salutary effect. The
leaves used have a eucalyptus flavour; some are chewed, others are
rubbed on. To cure localised pains a diseased limb will often be
ligatured with a cord. In the case of a headache, some incisions
may be made on the forehead with the aid of a glass splinter or a
shell, which are then rubbed with ginger. *Gentye* has nothing to do
with the *yevale*, and consequently provides no occasion for calling
in a medicine-man or using magical cures. It is not unlikely, however, that, depending on the gravity of the indisposition, some of
the dietary restrictions which are normally connected with serious
illness are observed, such as the eating of young palm-leaf shoots
and the abstention from meat (though not the flesh of birds, sago

worms, and so on).

Serious illnesses other than epidemic diseases (*akone*) are either *arga seráuw* or *nakyasub*. Both are sent by the *yevale* in punishment of offences committed. The symptoms of *arga seráuw* are stinging, localized pains, swellings, and so on. They are caused by one of the *song* (bamboo) *yevale*, Yake and Kánkonan.

> *Editor's comment.* The translation of *song* with bamboo is dubious. *Song* also, if not primarily, denotes the bamboo knife used by the headhunter to cut a victim's throat (Marind: *sok*). This explains the reference to Yake, who elsewhere in the text is mentioned as the first (mythical) headhunter. Further information on Kánkonan is not available.

Nakyasub are all those illnesses which, though initially they sometimes resemble *arga seráuw*, cannot be cured by conventional means, and finally exhaust the patient to such an extent that he becomes weak and apathetic, going about with hanging head. A man who walks face down is suffering from the most dangerous of all illnesses, *nakyasub*.

That both forms of serious illness are considered as punishment for immoral or foolish behaviour is well illustrated by the admonition which older men used to give their children: "Never beat or stab another person, and do not unnecessarily become involved in a major row, lest Yake assail you as a result. Do not kill a tribal fellow, for Kánkonan will punish you. And do not take another man's wife or garden produce, because Baderam will enter you." (Baderam is the *yevale* responsible for sending *nakyasub*.) A cure must be achieved by means of magic in either case.

If a man fears that he has been stricken with *arga seráuw*, he will send his wife to their garden to fetch kava. Then a medicine-man will be called in. The patient will prepare kava, which is kept on hand nearby, when the medicine-man arrives. The latter will drink of it and sit down. When the kava begins to take effect, he will arise, go to the patient, and blow in his ears. Then he gives him a massage, beginning with the head. Gradually, he descends to the aching spot, which, of course, the patient has already indicated to him. Once the healer feels he has hit the right spot, he grasps it firmly and pulls at it till, suddenly loosening his grip, he throws a blood-stained piece of bamboo or rattan onto the mat next to the patient. Then he takes a pair of fire-tongs with which he picks up the blood-stained object, and deposits it carefully somewhere above the fire, where it will be able to dry quickly. When the blood has dried up, the patient will be cured. Usually the mere sight of the bloody object will suffice to alleviate the patient's pains. He may feel sick for another few days, but the cure is allegedly infallible. In practice it never occurred that a patient died after such treatment, unless, as was sometimes the case, it turned out that the patient also suffered from *nakyasub*.

Nakyasub is the more serious kind of illness. Being caused by Baderam, a female *yevale*, the sickness is also called the female sickness (not to be confused with venereal disease, although venereal granulome is also ascribed to Baderam). To cure this illness, a medicine-man is called in just as in the case of *arga se-ráuw*. He will make his diagnosis whilst massaging the patient. Moving in a downward direction all over the sufferer's body, he will finally tell his patient: "There is nothing here, but inside your body the flesh is curled up and turned inside out. You have the illness of Baderam." If the medicine-man is an *arga seráuw* specialist, he will go home without having achieved anything. Each medicine-man's power is restricted to one special *yevale*. Another one will now be called in, one who is able to cure *nakyasub*. For him again kava is prepared, and again the treatment begins with blowing in the patient's ears. This is done either to blow the patient's sleeping vital spirit awake, or, if the spirit should have tried to make off through the ears, to blow it back into the body.

The medicine-man then seats himself next to the patient and says: "Baderam has stricken you. You must have committed some sin. Tell them." The patient must then confess, more or less in the same way as the woman in labour whose case was discussed above (Chapter III, pp. 32-33). The brushing of the patient with a twig and the for-mulas used are the same, but the procedure which follows is dif-ferent. Whereas the pregnant woman pushes out the baby herself, the patient's sickness must be fetched by the healer. Towards this end the medicine-man takes a one-fathom-long cord. One end of the cord is placed under the patient's tongue - just for him to swallow, people say. The medicine-man makes a few rapid gestures with his hands, and then one of swallowing, and suddenly the cord has dis-appeared - obviously under the hairlengthenings or the armpits of the medicine-man, who states: "The cord is now on its way to fetch the patient's illness". He quietly squats down at a short distance, from where he is able to observe the patient, as the cord must have sufficient time to tie the spirit of illness. Then he goes back to the patient for the usual massage. Suddenly the medicine-man claps both hands together. When he opens them again, the cord of a few moments ago is back in its place, with a miniature *sinák* (women's apron) tied to it. The medicine-man now leaps to his feet to cast the *sinák* into a fire, where it is burnt.

If the patient does not recover after this treatment, the medi-cine-man will admit that he has not been able to catch the whole *sinák*, a small part of it having slipped from his hands. For the patient this means the end. It is the really finishing blow. The medicine-man's failure cannot be made good. The remaining piece of *sinák* has become too wise to allow itself to be caught by the healer's cord a second time.

Editor's comment. Before proceeding to the discussion of epidemic disease (*akone*), some comment is called for on three points, namely: both the similarity and difference between the case of the woman in labour and that of the man suffering from *nakyasub*; the similarity and difference between *nakyasub* and *arga seráuw*; and the possibility of other forms of illness being inflicted, alongside *nakyasub* and *arga seráuw*, through the medium of *yevale*. For the sake of clarity it is best to begin with the contrast and similarity between *arga seráuw* and *nakyasub*, which, to all appearances, refers to a basic opposition, that between the sexes.

The admonition given by the older people to youngsters (above) makes a clear distinction: *arga seráuw* is a punishment for public offences (beating, fighting and killing), and *nakyasub* for secret private sins (adultery and theft). According to a communication by Verschueren elsewhere in his papers, the latter sins are essentially identical, adultery being just a form of theft. The contrast public versus secret helps to clarify an annoying obscurity in Verschueren's presentation of the facts. In ms. A we are told that in every case of serious illness the success of the patient's treatment depends upon his confession of errors committed. Nevertheless, ms. B does not devote a single word to confession in the case of *arga seráuw*, and confines itself to mentioning it as part of the treatment for *nakyasub*. It is evident that ms. B is more correct on this point than the generalizing argumentation of ms. A. Public offences and sins do not need to be confessed, as everyone knows about them. It is only in case of secret wrongdoings that confession is called for.[1] Unfortunately we are not told what the social consequences of such a confession are. Nothing is said about the reactions of the offended party. We must content ourselves with the fact that secret sins are connected with the female sex and with deadly peril, an association noted already in our discussion of Atu, *konan* and the death-inflicting *kupe* (Chapter IV, Section 7). The fact that the illness of Baderam is explicitly called the female illness strongly supports this association of the female sex with secret sin and deadly peril.

By contrast, *arga seráuw* is not identified in so many words as a male illness, though its association with the bamboo headhunters' knife certainly points in this direction. The alternative of a bamboo splinter, a piece of rattan extracted by the medicine-man from his patient's body, can also be interpreted as a reference to headhunting; the shaft of the club, the warrior's weapon, is usually made of rattan. The association of *arga seráuw* with public violence again confirms its association with the male sex, as does the firm conviction that it is always a curable disease. The medicine-man is an *orei-kerau*, or *orei*-man, who is masculinity incarnate. And in this context it is fascinating to give some attention to the ultimate cause of death where the treatment of the illness of Baderam is unsuccessful: in that case a piece of a woman's apron has remained behind in the victim's body. Apparently things female are poisonous to a man. And of course they are; every initiate must become *orei* (above, p. 62).

There is more still to be said on this point. When a woman in labour is stricken by Baderam, a confession of sexual sins (adultery) is sufficient to make the baby emerge, but in the case of a man the illness must be extracted by means of a cord held under the patient's tongue. This reminds us of the *kupŏr* held under the tongue of the neophyte by the older initiates. They, too, are *orei*-men, and consequently medicine-men. Would it be going too far to equate the cord with an umbilical cord and thus interpret the act as another case of appropriation of typically female features by males?

Finally, we must consider the possibility that, in addition to
arga seráuw and *nakyasub*, other *yevale*-caused illnesses may occur
which do not fall in the category of epidemic diseases. The fact
is that Verschueren's report on sickness and healing is obviously
incomplete. Apart from the references to the woman in labour, his
data are concerned with male patients only. Do male medicine-men
also treat women, and if so, are women prone to the same kinds
of illnesses as men? It is highly improbable that a woman would
be as badly injured by a piece of apron in her system as a man.
And *arga seráuw* does not very well fit in with the life conditions of a female. Or are there other female diseases? And are
they treated by female healers? We simply do not know.

What we do know from ms. A is that other objects than those
connected with *arga seráuw* and *nakyasub* are occasionally extracted from a patient's body. The ms. mentions an arrow-point, a pig's
tooth and a stone, none of which fits in the context of either of
the two major diseases as perfectly as the bamboo splinter and
the women's apron. Besides, among the wrongdoings confessed in
the case of illness are mentioned such offences as the violation
of a taboo on eating meat, a man's entering the *wake*, and irrev-
erent behaviour vis-à-vis *komen* or *yevale*.

The fact that in each case a specific *yevale* may feel offended
suggests that he will use his own methods for taking revenge,
methods for which he does not need the intervention of either
the *song-yevale* or Baderam. Greater variety is also suggested
by the fact that every *orei*-man has his own *yevale* (above, page
62, note 6, and page 69) and that the united *orei*-men of a
settlement appeal to the entire body of *yevale* of their *arow*
(below). Unfortunately, we do not know how all this works. We
even do not know whether Baderam as a female is a Telle and the
song-yevale a Nak *yevale*, which would involve having repeatedly
to call a medicine-man from another than the patient's settlement. However, there is no sense in speculating on this. We must
now turn to the remaining forms of illness and healing reported
in ms. B.

A final form of illness is that of epidemic disease, *akone*. Even
the senior men are not quite certain whether *akone* is the *yevale*
himself or simply his work. The one thing they know for sure is
that he cannot be one of "our" *yevale*. He comes from afar, very far
indeed, unleashed by no one knows who or where. But the *orei-kerau*
(medicine-men) know long in advance when he is on his way. Their
eyes have been opened by *köllu-köllu*. They will brush the entire
settlement with a duster of cassowary feathers, invoking all the
yevale of their *arow* to help them find the *akone* and drive him
away to a distant, hostile area such as that of the Boadzi or the
upper Bian. Then they will close the entrance ways to the settlement. They will say to their people: "Well, it is safer to outwit
'that thing'. Perhaps our *yevale* will not be able to stop it." Then
all the members of the settlement will disperse over the entire
surroundings, splitting up into separate family groups. Every sound
must be stricly avoided. Drums are prohibited. When beating sago,
the women must add more water to the pulp than is usual in order

to deaden the sound. In the meantime the *orei-kerau* occasionally
sneak stealthily back to the village. There they can hear the disease, and report: "He is roaming about in the village. He is spit-
ting and calling: 'Bah, where are these chaps, those cowards?' ".
Sometimes his calling can be heard at an hour's distance. When at
last an *orei*-man feels sure that the disease has departed for another village, he will go around and report: "It is light again
now (i.e. no longer dark with disease); let us return to the settlement". Silently, and without any feasting, they come back to the
village one after the other.

Finally, there is yet another, quite different cure against illness. The patient (or, if he is unable to walk, a member of his
family) will go to the *yevale* of his *mother* to drink from a well
or brook in the immediate vicinity of its residence. He will wash
and bathe there, saying: "*Yevale*, I have come hither to be cured
by you".

Editor's comment. The concluding statement concerning the healing
power of one's mother's *yevale* is more than a reconfirmation of
the close relations prevailing between the *jéi* of a mother's
brother and that of his sister's children. It underlines the fact
that each clan has its special *yevale*, which is also reflected in
the *orei*-men's invoking the combined *yevale* of their *arow* to protect them against the *akone*, and in the repeated statement that
a medicine-man (or *orei*-man, initiate - the terms are identical)
only has powers over his own *yevale*. The data presented do, in
fact, suggest that every initiate is a medicine-man with respect
to matters concerning his clan *yevale*. This does not exclude the
possibility that one medicine-man will be a better expert than
the other, nor that the range of activities of the one will be
wider than that of the other. But the data are too vague for us
to be able to make a really definite statement about the inter-
relation between the initiate, medicine-man, clan totem and clan
yevale or about the function of moiety dualism in the classifica-
tion of the various forms of disease. One thing is obvious, however. The eyes of the *orei-kerau*, or *orei*-men, "have been opened
by *köllu-köllu*" (above), which statement may be supplemented with
the words "by swallowing the *kupör* alias *orei*". As "every medicine-man's power is restricted to one special *yevale*" (p. 69),
which cannot be any other than his personal, i.e. his *jéi's*
yevale, the assumption seems justified that the *kupör* swallowed
is to be identified with the *kupör* given to the relevant *yevale*
by Orei. In our discussion of the scene around the menstruation
hut, the final scene of the *köllu-köllu*, we noted that it is a
reflection of that of the returning war party at the *konan* with
the aim of planting the shaft of the *pöggul* (see page 64).
Would it really be too bold a speculation to suggest that the
initiate/medicine-man is the reincarnation of his clan *yevale*,
who left the *orei*-tree or -canoe with his *kupör* in his hand? If
this is correct, then Yéi-nan totemism must have been ritually
more important than we have hitherto supposed, which importance
does not derive from its forming part of a ritual drama of the
kind enacted in a Marind-anim rite, but from the power of the

magical act performed by an initiate who has become one with Orei
by swallowing the *kupör*, which is the *kupör* of his clan and
yevale. This phallic symbol is the repository of all magic power,
and its manipulation in the acts of the *orei*-man fully corroborates the conclusion at which we arrived at the end of the previous chapter, namely that the phallic symbolism of the Yéi is
more explicit than that of the Marind.

Chapter VII

Death, Burial, and Mortuary Feasts

1. Death

According to the old men the ultimate cause of death is offences committed by the people themselves. They thereby incur the wrath of the *yevale* and thus invite their own ruin. Really old people are rare. The saying is that they are "like a *tsölluk* tree[1], of which in the end, however, the boughs are broken (= his children are dead) and which will not be able to stand for much longer". In such a case no one associates death with punishment. Such a man's penis shell just hangs there uselessly. His virility has gone, his boughs are broken. Sometimes his brains will rattle in his head. When such a person shakes his head, you are able to hear it, they say. Usually, however, death comes earlier, and always as a punishment for sins committed, sins against which the old rarely tire of warning rebellious youngsters.

The myths express a different opinion on the origin of death. In Kwél the following story was told:
The story took place in Kalót on the Obat River. The boy was but small and his father had gone out hunting. He was alone with his mother, and wept. His mother tried everything to soothe him. But he did not want sago ... and he did not want meat ... and he did not want fish ... and he went on and on crying. Then his mother became angry and called out: "What do you want, then? Do you want this?", and she showed him her vulva, which was as wide as the mouth of a sago-bag. Suddenly the boy stopped weeping. He was satisfied [i.e. he satisfied himself]. He carried on so violently, that he ruined his mother's pudenda, and they became very small. When the father came home, the woman complained: "Look what the boy has done to me". When the father saw this, he became very angry and said: "Wait and see". And he made a snake.

He made different snakes. First he made the non-dangerous kinds, but finally he made the *debola*, a short, black, and extremely dangerous species. He cut his snakes out of different kinds of wood, but made the *debola* out of *debol* and painted it. Then he let the snake loose, but every time he called the snake, the animal came back to him. He then took it to a large tree in which many small birds were flitting, and said to the snake: "When he comes, bite him". Now he called his son and said: "See all the small birds! Take your little bow and arrows and shoot them!" The boy then took his small bow and went to the tree, where the snake bit him in both legs. Crying, he returned, calling: "Father, a snake bit me!" But none of the *orei kerau* could heal him, and he died. His corpse was taken to Un and buried in a narrow spit of land near the river. Ornamental shrubs were planted around it. Kossál is the name of the

place. People wept on the grave for three nights and three days,
and all the pigeons in the forest wept with them.

On the third day a few small boys were taking a bath in the river
nearby. The dead boy had emerged from the grave, and, seeing the
boys bathing, called for a canoe: *na kwor kenadere.*[2] On seeing him
standing on his grave, the boys took fright and ran back home. They
told their parents, who went out to take a look; and indeed, there
the boy stood, calling for a canoe. They went back to fetch a canoe,
but at the moment they reached the middle of the river a frog broke
the oar. They went back for another one, but again the frog broke
it, and so on time after time. And the boy waited but no-one arrived. Then he got angry and called out: "All right! You are not
coming to get me, but beware, you will all follow me. You will all
die, and in various ways". And he summed up all the various ways
in which people die. Then he took his drum and sang: *Oh wobene
kamean oh, nako dörkon oh* (I am going away, you will all follow me).
Then he hung his skin over the branch of a tree, took his drum, and
went.

And this is why all men must die. Otherwise, we would only have
had to change our skins, like a snake. And the old men add that,
long ago, they opened the grave and found it completely empty!

Editor's comment. Verschueren adds that the myth probably does
not confine itself to a description of the origin of death (in
which respect it corresponds with the relevant myth of the Boadzi), but also tries to explain the origin of black magic. The
black snake made of wood which obeys its master (the *kupör*), the
place of the grave (*kossál*), the inability of the *orei kerau* to
heal the boy, and the latter's death in retaliation for an of-
fence committed are all symptomatic of sorcery.

In all this Verschueren is probably correct. In Marind-anim
myth the origin of death is also associated with the first act
of sorcery. Intriguing in Verschueren's comment is the snake's
relation with the *kupör*, the equivalent of the Marind-anim *tang*,
which also plays a part in lethal sorcery (*kambara*). Unfortunately, having no knowledge of the Yéi language, I have no idea what
the meaning of *kossál*, the name of the place where the boy was
buried, is. So I must restrict my comment to the indication that
apparently the *kupör* plays the same ambiguous role in Yéi religion as the bullroarer (and *tang*) in that of the Marind-anim,
namely as a life- as well as a death-bringing implement.[3]

The point is of all the greater interest because the story itself is unmistakably of the Oedipus type, and strongly emphasizes
the sexual character of Yéi-nan thinking.

To the Yéi-nan dying means that the soul (*nenge-nenge*) leaves the
body, this time forever. During life the same thing may happen when
a person dreams, but then the *nenge-nenge* (there is only one term
for soul, both before and after death) returns before the person
awakes. After death the soul lingers in the neighbourhood of the
settlement, in the nearby bush. There, where the bush begins, the
relatives of the deceased prepare a spot where all the things are
collected which, before the grave in the house was closed, they have

presented to the deceased as articles which he may need in the here-
after, saying: "Here is this and here is that. Do not cause us any
further trouble". Trouble is what people fear most from the dead.
They want them to go, and the entire mourning ritual is directed
to that goal. Not that the dead are considered especially dangerous, but simply uncanny, so that they must be kept away from the
company of the living. Occasionally people have an encounter with
a soul, which encounters are always eery. They are a favourite
topic of conversation and discussion. The only souls which do not
cause trouble are those of people who have died in combat. Their
souls ascend straight to the sky, above the clouds, in the direction of the sun. [To what ultimate destination the other souls go
the author does not say.]

If possible, a dying person is conveyed to the settlement before he
dies, as the corpse must be taken there anyway. When death is immi-
nent, his relatives, including in-laws and relatives in the female
line, are hastily warned. They should all have a final opportunity
of seeing the dying person. When a man is on the point of death,
his wife will fling herself on his body, at one time acting as
though dead, at another raving like a mad person.

2. Burial

After death, the deceased's body is painted all over. Children are
blackened with charcoal; young, marriageable persons are painted
with red ochre; married people with yellow clay; and old, infirm
people again are blackened with charcoal, the men with a few bars
of white clay across their chest, arms and legs. Corpses are always
placed in a supine position and then decorated. Often a young coconut tree and a banana tree owned by the deceased will be cut down
as a sign of mourning. The occasional killing of a pig (cf. Chapter
VIII, Section 2) will be postponed till the mourning ceremony.
   In the meantime members of another than the deceased's descent
group will dig the grave. It will be located in the women's part
of the communal house, quite close to the central pole with the
headhunting trophies. The grave-diggers make sure that any roots of
trees and shrubs which they happen to encounter are removed and
eliminated in such a way that they cannot be put back into the
grave. The time of burial is not a fixed one but it is always as
soon as possible after death, and preferably in the late afternoon.
   During the digging of the grave the relatives will collect the
deceased's implements as well as some of his garden crops. They
will roast sago on the fire used by him before his death, and put
some raw sago in a basket. If the deceased is a married man, some
pieces of roofing will be put in readiness; he may need these to
build a house. Meanwhile the deceased has been placed in the grave
on his own sleeping-mat. His mouth, nose, ears and eyes are covered
with a banana-leaf to keep the sand out. Now his next-of-kin will
arrive, bringing with them all the things they have collected for
him, such as his tools, the sago, etc. One by one these objects are
taken to the grave and mentioned by name, viz.: "This is your axe",
etc. But they are not put in the grave but are taken to a special-

ly prepared place at the edge of the nearby bush. Immediately after
this the grave is closed. On top, right above the deceased's chest,
a piece of eucalyptus bark is spread, and then the whole thing is
covered with a *wontye*, a *nibung* flower-spathe or a discarded mourning-hood used as a sleeping-mat.

After the burial the widow, mother, or other close female relative will put on her mourning-dress and sit down on top of the
grave. The relevant mourning-garments and adornments are:
the *köbbu*, a large, wide mourning-hood of plaited fibres, which
covers the entire face [actually the entire body, cf. the Editor's
comment below];
the *mombute*, a kind of jacket which covers the chest and is also
plaited of bark (fibres);
the *dibár*, a kind of skirt or *sinak*, made up of a large number of
suspended cords with at the lower end big tassels of fibre;
the *malusu*, plaited armlets with tassels;
the *worgi*, plaited leg-bands with tassels;
the *dörkodörgi*, strings with tassels suspended from the ears;
the *tangge gi*, a string with tassels suspended from the nose.

All the deceased's relatives rub their bodies with white clay and
don the mourning-dress or *soya*. The *soya* varies in complexity, depending on the degree of the wearer's relationship to the deceased.
There are also differences according to sex. The principal (and
most complete) *soya* includes the large and the small *köbbu* along
with all the items mentioned above. The males, however, do not
wear a *köbbu*, but a plaited round cap (*kirkébu*) adorned with tassels which hang down at the back. The second *soya* is made up of the
small *köbbu*, the armlets and leg-bands, a necklace, and a wrist-
band. The third *soya* is restricted to the small *köbbu* only. It is
worn by close friends and distant relatives. For the next of kin
the adoption of the *soya* implies the beginning of a period of seg-
regation and fasting during which bathing and fishing are forbidden.

Editor's comment. Verschueren's description of the highly complex
mourning-dress is too brief to give an idea of the impression it
creates. Besides, it is incomplete, and, as far as one detail is
concerned, incorrect. A comparison with the data presented by the
Mission teacher Renwarin and with Fig. 1 of his diagram (Plate I)
shows that Verschueren omitted the *kamartye*, the breast-cloth
worn by both men and women, which *kamartye* - and not the small
köbbu - is the distinctive mourning-sign of the small (third)
soya worn by friends and distant relatives. Actually, no *köbbu*,
not even the small one, could serve this purpose, as it cannot
be worn by men; its use is exclusive to women only. Renwarin's
contributions at the same time provide a welcome illustration of
the variations in the vocabulary and phonemic system of the Yéi-
nan language. Apparently not all spelling differences (such as
Wirz's *kabu* over against Renwarin's *kéboe* for *köbbu*) are attributable to differences in these authors' spelling systems.

More detailed information on the mourning-dress is furnished
by Wirz (1925(III):134f. and the figures of Tafel 14-16) and
Nevermann 1942:166-9. These sources show that the small *köbbu* is

a beautifully plaited hood which hangs down from the head to the
knees. Its lower edge is adorned with tassels (not mentioned by
Renwarin) which drop down to just above the ground. The big *köbbu*
is wider, so wide that it can easily be wrapped around the front
of the body as well. At the top there is a cross-piece which
covers the greater part of the wearer's face, so that she can only
see the ground just in front of her feet. The garment provides
an effective impediment to all her movements. The reader, when
consulting the sources quoted above, should allow for the occurrence of local differences.

Nevermann's account presents a number of other interesting details. In his comment on the fact that a widow must sleep on her
late husband's grave, he states: "She has to listen whether the
deceased speaks to her. He is expected to whisper to her who has
killed him. Usually, the woman will quite soon report that the
deceased has pointed to a certain person as the one who is responsible for his death. The male members of the deceased's totem
clan will then take revenge, either through sorcery or through
an act of violence. Men whose son has died will go into the forest, taking the skull of a beheaded person with them, and there
adjure a snake to give the murderer a lethal bite" (p. 167). This,
of course, provides strong support for my assertion that sorcery
does occur among the Yéi (above, Chapter VI). Nevertheless, it
was not put forward there as a relevant argument for the simple
reason that its authenticity is not beyond doubt. Nevermann must
have received his information from a mission teacher, these
teachers being his main informants during his three-week tour, or
from a missionary. Many of these were more conversant with Marind-
anim customs than with the Yéi-nan culture. They must have known
that sleeping on a grave for this purpose (but here by a man) was
not uncommon among the Marind (Van Baal 1966:681, 683). An interpretation of the Yéi-nan custom with a widow as medium in terms
borrowed from a well-known Marind-anim practice is not impossible. This does not exclude the possibility of Nevermann's information being correct; only, it should have been checked. But
Nevermann never checked any information. In the same context he
manages to assert that the (large) *köbbu* serves to conceal the
women from the spirits of the deceased, who are most dangerous
to those who are closest to them. And he does so without even for
a moment wondering why, of all places, the women dwell on the
grave.
    With Nevermann we never know where we stand, except when he is
telling what he himself really saw. Such is the case with the
report of his visit to a burial house. At the time of his stay
in the area, the dead were no longer buried in the communal
house, but in a separate burial house nearby. His description
suggests that this was an old communal house used especially for
this purpose ever since the government had forbidden burial of
the dead inside a house occupied by the living. Later (below) the
probability that this is not a new custom but an old one will be
discussed. But first we must return to Verschueren's text.

Immediately after the closing of the grave, the women who are next
of kin (including the widow, of course) seat themselves on the
grave. They are not allowed to leave it save in case of necessity,
and even then only by crawling. Meat and fish, and during the first
days even sago, are forbidden. The closest male relatives are subject to the same taboos. They remain in the *soama*, where they hurriedly make the ornamental arrows which will be needed a few days
later. Meanwhile, the women in the *wake* complete their mourning-
dress. Every morning a ceremonial wailing takes place, which lasts
from dawn till the sun is shining brightly. At five o'clock in the
afternoon the wailing is resumed and goes on until total dark.

Meanwhile the women of related groups from the opposite moiety
have arrived. [Many of these women are, of course, classificatory
sisters of the deceased.] For three consecutive days they will give
a performance representing the life of the deceased every morning
and afternoon. All of them have equipped themselves with male ornaments over their female dress (the apron): a pubic shell, hairlengthenings, bird of paradise feathers, and a bow and arrows. The
first day the women restrict themselves to following the nearby
paths which were frequently trodden by the deceased during his life-
time. They do so under continual wailing. The second day there is
no longer any wailing. They then put on a play, enacting episodes
from the successive periods of the deceased's life, from his youth
until his marriage. The third day is devoted to his life after his
marriage and until his death. All sorts of things are depicted by
the women: his hunting of pigs and cassowaries; feasts in which he
has participated; his manufacture of a canoe; headhunting raids
ending in the taking of a head by him (the head being represented
by a coconut), and so on.

The women's clumsy, untrained performance provides relaxation for
the bereaved, who cannot themselves participate anyway. The men are
constantly busy making arrows, the women completing their mourning-
dress. They soothe their hunger with bananas, yams and taro, but
not with sago.

On the fourth day the women of the opposite moiety go out to prepare sago. They select a very young tree, the pith of which must be
pounded in its entirety on that same day. Immediately after their
return to the settlement, the sago is put in bamboo cylinders and
roasted over a fire which is only now kindled next to the grave.
Until that moment the wailing women have stayed there in darkness.
A few married men then take the sago and hand it out one by one to
the women on the grave and the mourning men sitting nearby in the
soama. On presenting the sago they give the sitting mourners a
hand and slowly pull them up. This is the end of the taboo on
moving about and on eating sago.

Shortly afterwards [I presume on the fifth day, which is not specified in the papers] the men have an opportunity of planting their
yepe kweál, or ornamental arrows. They take the arrows, a bamboo
cylinder filled with lime, and a number of leaves (sirih or other
leaves). First of all they place some of the arrows in front of
members of the settlement who are not relatives. Then they proceed
to the various paths in the neighbourhood, and more specifically
to those which give access to the gardens and sago groves of the

deceased. Each time an arrow is planted by inserting the shaft into the ground lime is scattered over a few leaves. This is a sign that from now on the gardens and other belongings of the deceased are taboo (*walel*). No one will follow such a path, and if by chance anyone needs to go that way he will cut a new path nearby.

After these first five days, which end with the imposition of the *walel*, the women make an enclosure around the grave, on which, from now on, they need no longer stay. The fire next to it must, however, be kept burning and the women must see to it that it does not go out.

> *Editor's comment.* The enactment of scenes from the life of the deceased is always by women, even if the deceased is also a woman. However, as is only natural, this enactment is always restricted to the mortuary ceremonies for influential people.

3. Mortuary feasts

One or two months later the mourning-ceremony is held. Members of both moieties participate. The women pound sago and collect garden produce and *kava* and the men prepare an ample stock of ornamental arrows decorated with such designs as: ⚒ . When everything is ready and the guests are expected to arrive, the materials of the fire next to the grave are scattered over the mound. Then the ashes are taken to the edge of the nearby bush, where the gifts presented to the deceased at his burial have been assembled. The participants now return to the house, where they circle around the grave in silence and then sit down, each in his or her own place.

When the guests arrive, they all lament for a while before sitting down, the men in the *soama*, the women in the *wake*. The male guests have brought ornamental arrows, which are now exchanged for those of the hosts. That is the reason why so much care is devoted to their manufacture, an element of competition not being absent. Now a new, big fire is lighted next to the grave, this time to roast the food. This is the first time the hosts will eat meat and fish with their guests again. The deceased, too, receives his share. A piece of roasted sago is taken to "his" place at the edge of the bush.

After nightfall the men in the *soama* sing *kwanap*. They sit motionless around the big drums and sing all night through. In earlier days the Yéi had a special drum for *kwanap* singing, one decorated with a specific kind of carving, but such drums are no longer found today.

At the same time another ceremony is conducted in the *wake*. This is the *yagóne*, a dance performed by two actors, older men who are members of the guest group. Each has a pair of horns made out of wild beeswax on his head. From the back of their head hangs a long rope ending in a tassel of fibres of the *wasuk* (a water-lily). It almost reaches down to the ground. The two performers enter the *wake* and take up their position, facing each other, near the grave. They bend their knees in time with the melody of their song, making sure that their long tail sways forward between their legs at every bend. They distort their voices so that, as people say, these sound as hoarse and raucous as that of the bush bird.

The girls - those who have gone through the menstruation ceremony but have not yet been married - dance in a circle around them, holding one another by the shoulder. They reply to the song of the two men. I was able to note down a few lines of the *yagóne*, viz.:

Oh ah wale ah joal ah,	*wale* = a variety of yam?
Oh ah nepi ah nejib ah,	*nepi* = now
wali ah nepi ah,	*nejib* = cousin
Wah degigwa	*degigwa* = they sing (the women)

The melody of the song is as follows:

1 . .7̄ 5 . . .6̄ 5 . . 0   1̄ . .7̄ 5 . . .3̄ 5 . . 0

It is worth pointing out that what happens here is the exact reverse of the procedure followed on the occasion of the *köllu-köllu* ritual, the celebration of a girl's first menstruation. There the *orei*-men danced around the girl, here the girls dance around the *orei*-men. [*Orei* is, of course, what the two old men are.]

No one was able to explain the meaning of the horns (called *tajam* or *marenge*). They are not worn at *köllu-köllu* performances, they say (?). The performance by two old men is explained in Erambu, Kwél and Bupul as a reference to Nak and Telle, because one of the two must be Nak, the other Telle. In Polka it was stated, however, that there could be several male dancers [thus implicitly denying the reference to Nak and Telle]. In Polka it was also explained that the horns have been borrowed from the Kanum people, where, in fact, the spirits of the dead are represented as wearing horns (which I checked on at Yanggandur on February 18, 1954).[4] There is yet another difference between the southern and the northern Yéinan. Among the southern groups the *yagóne* is danced in the *soama*, the *kwanap* in the *wáke*, the exact reverse of what happens among the northern Yéi.

The celebration has come to an end with the two dances just described. Some of the more distant relatives now take off their *soya* (mourning-dress) and hang it above the grave. The great *soya*, however, which is worn by the closer relatives of the deceased, is kept on. The *walel* (taboo on the gardens) is also maintained.

Finally, it is the custom for people to avail themselves of the opportunity presented by a burial to send small presents to mourned relatives who have passed away previously. For this purpose a small package is made, filled with some kava, betel or other suchlike things, and provided with a distinctive badge, a *maker*. The package is placed at the spot at the edge of the bush where the presents given to the newly deceased have been assembled. The latter is supposed to be kind enough to pass it on to the beloved deceased in the nether world.

Editor's comment. This latter addition to the text is of great interest. These *maker*, to which Verschueren does not give any further attention, have been described and illustrated by Nevermann, who devoted some eight pages of his work to them (1942:174-82). His conclusion that they all refer to the totem of either the giver or the recipient is sufficiently substantiated by the facts which he has put forward. Of course, they tell us little

about the religious content of Yéi-nan totemism, but make it no
longer possible to deny that clan identity is expressed through
symbols which in every respect resemble totems.

Highly interesting also is Verschueren's observation that the
male dancers of the *yagóne* are *orei*. At the *köllu-köllu*, a ceremony celebrating the manifestation of fertility in a girl, the
orei were dominant and circled around the girl's refuge. Here,
in the face of death, the girls are dominant and circle around
the *orei* near the grave. The phallic symbolism recurs in every
situation. It does here, too, and is not restricted to the *yagóne*,
whatever the specific meaning of this. It is also present in the
arrows exchanged with the guests and distributed among the un-
related males of the deceased's settlement. Their symbolism, it
seems, combines the life-giving potency of the males with the
death-bringing power of their weapons. To say more about this
would be absurd. It is the nature of symbols to express the in-
expressible.

A year or more later follows the final feast, the *feast of the
graves*. It serves the purpose of lifting the *soya* and the *walel*
(the taboo on the gardens). It is a really big feast, in which all
the neighbouring settlements participate. For this reason it is
often postponed until there are several deceased to commemorate
collectively.

The community first builds a new house, which is constructed at
the side of a road (trail) which has until then been tabooed by a
walel. Sometimes it is erected in a tabooed coconut garden. When
the house is finished the members of the mourning family clear
first the road and then the coconut garden. Then, for the first
time since the imposition of the *walel*, they roast sago in the re-
opened coconut grove. Subsequently, the other tabooed roads and
gardens are cleared. In this same period the mourners begin to re-
furbish their old ornaments, such as arm- and leg-bands, and pound
sago, fetch kava and garden produce, and prepare for the coming
feast.

Before the arrival of the guests (who will go straight to the new
building) a celebration takes place in the old house. Here a cross-
beam has been placed in position alongside the grave almost two
metres above the ground. During the night the wailing and singing
women will cling to this. Toward sunset a general wailing sets in.
Some women walk about in male attire. As soon as darkness falls,
however, the women assemble round the grave. They cling to the
cross-beam with both hands. Some of them wail, others strike up the
song *yerri abĕre*, which is sung by women only. The men keep silent
and all through the night hold up torches around the women, who,
clinging to the cross-beam, continue singing. Other women, who do
not take part in the singing, occasionally refresh them with water
or betel. The singing gradually increases in volume. When dawn approaches the women all of a sudden let go of the cross-beam and
fall to the ground on their haunches. This is the end of the ceremony. Everyone takes off his (her) *soya*. The best pieces are preserved, the others burnt. All sit down to eat and drink. Then they
rise in a body. Everyone takes his (her) belongings and departs for

the new house. The burial house is abandoned to decay in time.
   Now the second part of the ceremony begins in the new house. It
always consists of a meal, and often also of a ritual taking possession of the house. Its construction has been executed without
any ceremony or ritual, but the erection of the pole with the heads
in the centre of the house demands special attention. This pole
cannot be installed before the house has been finished. The pole
does not need to be carved or painted. The only requisite is that
it have a number of branches. Once it has been set up, the heads
and bones suspended from the pole in the old house are cleaned,
washed, and fastened to a new rattan. The jaws are kept apart, and
are tied to a rattan rope, one under the other. The bones, too, are
washed afresh. Then, without further ceremony, everything is suspended from the new pole. Finally, a new *kupör* is inserted into the
ground beside the pole. The next day everyone adorns him(her)self
and, for the first time in more than a year, there is *bendol* (a
dance). The ceremony is concluded with a communal meal. The widow
is taken back home by her relatives. If she has small children, she
may take these with her. The other children remain with the relatives of their deceased father. And life resumes its normal course
without anyone paying any further serious attention to the deceased.

4. Editor's comment

Verschueren's account is marred by certain gaps and inconsistencies which need to be discussed. First among these is the apparent discrepancy between the importance and scope of the rites
and the absence of any signs of worship of or communication with
the dead. This, however, is not necessarily a contradiction. The
same phenomenon is to be observed in the Marind-anim mortuary
rites, of which loving commemoration of the deceased is the central feature. The pantomimes performed by the visiting women a
few days after death suggest that similar ideas prevail among the
Yéi. All the same, we are told too little about their beliefs in
an afterlife; the information on this point is restricted to the
statement that the soul of a warrior who has died in battle goes
straight to the sky (Section 1, above) and the reference to the
custom of charging a recently deceased with the responsibility
for the transfer of gifts to mourned relatives who have departed
this life some time earlier in the past (Section 3, above). It
is this custom in particular which suggests that there is more
to death than is related here.
   A more serious shortcoming is the lack of information concerning the burial of children, women and persons of little consequence. Must these all be buried in the *wake* as well? What taboos
are observed in their case and what is the duration of the mourning period here? These questions are not unimportant, first and
foremost because in these regions, where many people die at an
early age, the *wake* might soon be full of graves. They are important in the second place because the necessity of removing the
house to another site after one or more burials implies so much
discontinuity, unrest and physical effort that a tendency to postpone the ceremony of the graves for as long as is humanly possible

would be almost inevitable. The communal houses of the Yéi may be fairly simple structures, but it is hardly conceivable that the occupants would be inclined to move more than once every five years.

The really important point, however, is that the end of the mourning period is dependent on the performance of the ceremony of the graves, i.e., on the removal to a new house. For a widow whose husband has died shortly after such a removal to a new house, this would imply a mourning period of some four years, and perhaps even longer. For her, the only way out is elopement with a young man, a solution about which we remarked earlier (Chapter III, Section 2, note 1) that it cannot have been as rare as Verschueren suggests. But it is not only widows who suffer under a prolonged mourning period. It also affects men, and not only a few of them, but all the male occupants of the house. At the end of the preceding section it was mentioned that at the entry into a new house the men sing *bendol* for the first time since the beginning of the mourning period. Besides, there are the tabooed coconut gardens and sago groves to consider. There may be many of these since the occurrence of the first death in the now discarded communal house! In settlements consisting of a number of small clan-community houses this situation may be tolerable for some, but in cases where the communal house counts a hundred or so residents, such as in Bupul in 1908 (Chapter II, Section 1), it would most certainly be unbearable. These Bupul men could hardly ever have sung *bendol* on any other occasion than the performance of a ceremony of the graves.

In the face of these facts one can only hypothesize that the ceremony of the graves was just one among various ways of winding up a mourning period. Such a hypothesis becomes the more likely if we accept that the old discarded house remains in use as a burial house, a supposition which is strongly corroborated by Nevermann's observations (Section 2, above). This implies that, following the removal to a new house, new deceased will be buried in the discarded house. This may go on until such time as the new house has been standing long enough for the desirability of constructing a new one to be considered. In preparation for this event, new burials will no longer be performed in the burial house, but in the way described above, amongst the living in the present communal house. This would provide an opportunity for certain families to put off their mourning at an earlier and more convenient time and thus for the male community as a whole to be absolved from the obligation to observe all the mourning taboos for each individual member.

This would, of course, also result in a shorter period of mourning for widows. Nevertheless, this might still be long enough to make elopement attractive. The widows' mourning-dress is so elaborate and, above all, is prepared with so much care and artistry as to be incompatible with its use for only a short time. It is the inferior social position of Yéi-nan women which is decisive. Their mourning-dress is not merely fine-looking, it is also cumbersome to a high degree. They are obliged to put on a show of lasting love which has no basis in the realities of their married

life, which is neither introduced by a period of courtship nor
enhanced by a satisfactory relationship with their husbands. Their
situation is such that, for widows at least, a long mourning
period seems probable in any case.

Chapter VIII

Other Ceremonies

1. The ceremony of the new canoe

Canoes are simple, moderately sized dug-outs, characterized by their pointed stem. Every canoe is made by the owner himself and is his personal property. To that end he or his father will have marked a tree growing somewhere in the territory of his *jéi*. When it has reached the appropriate size for the making of a canoe he will cut it down. He then works the trunk where it has fallen, till it has acquired its proper shape. Then he will cut a trail to the nearest river or swamp along which the canoe may be towed to the water. Canoe-making always takes place in the rainy season [or at least: the completion of a canoe] because then there is not much work left to do in the gardens and, most importantly, then there is water nearby almost everywhere, a circumstance which makes for shorter towage.

When everything is ready to start towing, the owner will collect food and kava and invite his friends from the same *arow* [N.B. *arow*, not *jéi*!] to assist him in pulling the canoe out of the forest. They are joined by the women, who will participate in the pulling. Together they proceed to the site of the dug-out, where a ceremony takes place. First the canoe is painted all over with red ochre. Then the medicine-man (*orei-kerau*) of the group comes forward, carrying a bow and arrow in his hand. Imitating shooting motions, he runs around the canoe a few times. Then he kicks with his foot against its stem and stern. Finally, he cleans the inside of the vessel with a brush of cassowary feathers, muttering: "Get out; return ye to thy own place. Do not obstruct the canoe!" Any *yevale* who might have taken refuge in the canoe is thus chased back to his own place.

The men now all stand around the canoe, each with a stick in his hand. Rhythmically beating their sticks on the sides of the canoe, they sing:

0 5	5.. $\overline{6}$	$\overline{7 6}$	5..	$\overline{5 5}$	$\overline{5 2}$..	.2	5..	$\overline{6 5}$	2..
Bál	*oh, Bál*	*ah-*	*oh,*	*ulib*	*ah,*	*Bál*	*eh,*	*oh Bál*	*ah.*

The owner of the canoe does not take part in the singing, but we are told that, on hearing it, he weeps with emotion. After the singing they all join hands, and the canoe is towed off to the settlement amid great merriness.

Editor's comment. One would have expected it to be taken to the waterside instead of the settlement. However, the remainder of Verschueren's description of the process clearly concerns a canoe cut from a tree which stood in the forest at the rear of the

settlement, not very far away from it. Therefore it was taken
straight to the settlement and, as will appear presently, placed
somewhere in the open space in front of the *soama*.

Once the canoe has arrived in the settlement, the owner will invite
his relatives from the opposite moiety [primarily his mother's
brother's kinsmen, and probably also the relatives of his in-laws.
Verschueren elucidates the point by adding that the owner invites
the nearest *arow* of the opposite moiety]. They will have the task
of decorating the stem of the canoe with carvings and seeing to its
final painting. Neither the owner of the canoe nor any of the men
of his moiety are allowed to do this. When all the work is completed both the guests and hosts retreat to the *soama*, where, toward
evening, they will sing *bendol*.
    The next morning the men assemble again at dawn. They have all
adorned themselves, and they proceed to the edge of the forest
singing *bendol*. They cry out the name of an enemy group, an act
which is explained as a request to their own *yevale* [apparently the
arow-yevale] to help them defeat these enemies. Then they all return to the *soama* in silence. Here the drums are stored away, and
they all sit down for a meal. During this meal they discuss the
details of the next ceremony, the actual launching of the canoe.
    The performers of this are the guests, the men from the opposite
moiety. They will tow the canoe to the waterside, where the hosts
have constructed a kind of triumphal arch by bending a tall bamboo
in a semi-circle and decorating it with young sago leaves. The
guests now assemble around the adorned canoe and sing *bál eh*. The
owner's mother's brother, imitating the part of a helmsman, seats
himself in front. Then the towing starts. They have to pass a small
hut made of leaves in which the mother's brother's son has concealed himself. As the towers approach, he emerges. He is decorated
all over. In his hands he holds a rattan loop of the kind used by
the Marind for catching pigs. From the loop hangs a gourd filled
with lime. He leaps forward, swinging the loop as though trying
to catch the canoe. Actually, he hits the stem of the vessel with
the gourd, which bursts open, scattering lime everywhere. Later he
will, in fact, catch the canoe through the loop, namely at the
point when its stem first touches the water. But the towers have
not yet advanced that far.
    They first have to pass under the arch near the waterside. Exact-
ly under the centre of the arch a big fire has been lighted, and the
canoe must pass straight through it. At the moment when the towers
have to watch their step lest they tread on burning twigs the hosts
pelt them with fire and big bush-ants and attack them with other
similar surprises. But as soon as they have passed through and the
canoe has been launched, the guests take revenge by throwing the
owner and all his relatives into the water. After thus squaring
accounts, the guests climb into the new canoe and row off. They
disappear around the nearest bend in the river. There they stop to
paint the sides of the canoe with black, grey and white mud and
loam lines. Then the crew is divided into two groups: oarsmen and
men who will beat a roll on the sides of the canoe with a short
stick in each hand. But before they depart the *gab-elul* comes for-

ward. He has a husked coconut in his hands, one of considerable
size. He sums up the names of all the persons he has killed, and
then hurls the coconut against the stem of the canoe with such
force that it splits open.

This is the signal for the return to the host settlement. The
rowers go as fast as they can. The men with the sticks beat a dull
ruffle on the sides of the canoe under a long-drawn-out shout of
éééééééh. As they approach the landing-place of the settlement,
their hosts welcome them with a protracted ááááááááh first and with
a shower of sticks next, which, duly reciprocated, only the more
adroit manage to evade. In the meantime the canoe proceeds at full
speed and runs up to the bank, landing between the spread legs of
the owner, who is standing there awaiting the return of his canoe.
They all disembark and the entire company returns to the settlement
to celebrate the end of the ceremony with a meal, kava-drinking,
and a sound nap.

One final remark that should be made is that the Yéi-nan do not
bestow proper names on their canoes like the Marind, who call them
after the *dema* of their cubclans.

2. *The pig-feast*

Like their neighbours, the Yéi-nan are pig-raisers from of old. Piglets were either caught in the bush or acquired from tame sows tended in the settlement. A pig was never tended by the man who had
caught or acquired it. If a Nak caught a piglet he would give it to
a Telle to raise, and vice versa. The name of the pig referred to
the identity of its owner. If a man of the Menakon-*jéi* caught a piglet, the pig was named Menakon-*jéi*, because the original owner retained his rights of property over it, though the pig was raised by
someone else.

The actual tending of a pig was a female task. As long as it was
still a piglet, the animal followed the woman who cared for it everywhere. Later, when it had grown bigger and might damage the gardens,
the pig would be transferred to an island or to the other side of
the river, where it could do no harm. There the woman in charge of
it would feed it every day. This went on for years, because it takes
quite a long time for a pig to grow sufficiently big and fat for
slaughtering. For this a festive occasion is needed. One would expect such a festive occasion to have been provided by a successful
headhunt or a big mourning ritual, but the Yéi-nan denied every
connection between a pig-feast and this kind of rituals, the one
exception admitted being the death of a pig-raising woman. The point
is that pigs are so attached to the women who care for them that
they may run wild if their personal tender is no longer there to
look after them. In such a case the mourning ritual held in the
woman's honour presented an appropriate opportunity for killing the
pig. However, this is an exception and not the true purpose of
raising pigs. This object is the feast connected with it, a feast
designed to strengthen the ties between *nêkèlè-biĕro*, or intermarrying groups. The latter statement is corroborated by the fact that
a man who has a piglet to give away preferably presents it to his
brother-in-law. This implies that the tender of the pig is, normal-

ly, the owner's sister.

Usually, several pigs were slaughtered at the same time. Once the members of a pig-raising group had decided to give a pig-feast, they would set out to construct as many pigsties as were needed. These were arranged in a row under a common roof. The Yéi did not follow the upper Bian custom of decorating pigsties; there was no carving of the poles, nor any painting or other forms of ornamentation. As soon as the sties were completed, the women lured their pigs to their respective sties, where they were locked up.

Now it was possible for a day to be fixed for the celebration. The prospective guests were informed of the exact day by means of a *tui* (Chapter III, page 28). In the meantime the women prepared sago for the feast. They stored the flour partly in *nibung* spathes, partly in large bags (*bögguteo*). Besides, one special *bögguteo* was put aside for each pig. It contained the sago, mixed with sago-leaves, in which in time the pig's head would be prepared. The men carried the necessary garden produce (mostly bananas) and kava to the settlement. And they constructed the platforms on which the pigs were to be carved up and distributed in front of the pigsties. These platforms were ornamented with croton and sago-leaves.

At this point the guests were expected. If the hosts were Nak, the guests would all be Telle. On the appointed day they would all arrive, festively adorned. They were lodged in open houses constructed at the edge of the bush. After nightfall, the feast would begin with a pantomime performed by two Telle men. They were guests, and as such were pig slaughterers. The one was styled *solo*, the other *boto*. Both were ornamented all over, with on their heads a long pliant twig with on top of it a feather. In the *solo*'s case this was a white cockatoo feather, in the *boto*'s a wooden representation of a stork feather. Both carried a drum, without, however, beating it. First came the *solo*. He was met by his sister, one of the pig-tending women. Facing her brother, she walked very slowly backwards, in one hand holding a torch, with the other scattering flowers and leaves in front of her brother's feet. Thus she led him from the guest pavilion to the house of the settlement. On arrival at the house, the *solo* would kneel and silently take off his headgear. His part had been played, and it was now *boto*'s turn to be led in exactly the same way by his sister from the pavilion to the house, where by this time the guests had started singing *bendol*. The hosts would not join in.

The next morning an *orei-kerau* (medicine-man) of the Nak (the hosts) would chase the *yevale* from the pigsties and the platforms facing it. Shouting and crying, he would beat the pigsties and platforms, and make shooting motions with his bow and arrow. When he had finished, the Telle would come forward and shoot the pigs with their arrows. The Nak would run away and their women start wailing, in which, once all the pigs had been killed, the Telle would join in. The suggestion that this wailing was meant for the dead was strongly rejected. The Nak women were simply bewailing their pigs, and the Telle were wailing out of sympathy with their sisters.

3. The inauguration of a new gab-elul

Long before the time has come for him to transfer his function to a
younger man, a good *gab-elul* will begin looking out for a worthy
successor among the younger men, including the bachelors. In consul-
tation with the older men, he selects a candidate who will from then
on be the object of his special attention. He passes on all his
knowledge to him, concentrating his instruction on matters connected
with warfare. As soon as he feels that the time is ripe, prepara-
tions are made for a big feast. An older man, an expert in the relevant technique, is invited to carve a new *pöggul*, the insignia of
his office.

On the day of the ceremony all the young men are summoned to the
space in front of the *soama*. Here the old *gab-elul* has taken up his
position, holding the new, beautifully decorated *pöggul* in both
hands. One by one the young men come forward. They touch the *pöggul*
with one hand and then run as fast as they can to a place some distance away (usually the *korár*) and back again to the point of departure. A man who does not run fast enough is jeered at. [Fast running
is essential. It is also mentioned in the myths (Chapter IV, Section
2).] When all the young men have demonstrated their ability, the candidate comes forward and touches the *pöggul* in just the same way as
the others. This time, however, the old *gab-elul* turns to him. He
carefully places the *pöggul* on the young man's shoulder with both
hands. The latter is now decorated on the spot with bird of paradise plumes, coloured clay, and ornamental leaves. His age-peers,
the runners in the preceding scene, stand around him. Stooping as
though burdened by the weight of the *pöggul* the candidate takes a
few steps and looks around as if in search of an enemy. Then suddenly the old *gab-elul* cries out: "There is the enemy". Instantly the
candidate runs off, followed by all his friends. On their return
to their starting-point, they find the old men and the ex-*gab-elul*
still leaping and shouting excitedly: "Catch him! Club him down!
Quick!"

When everyone is back in his place, the retiring headman address-
es his successor with the words: "I have observed you, and I accept
you as *gab-elul*. Take care to be a good man, so that there will be
no need for us to run away. A good headman never retreats. When
carrying the *pöggul* he can only advance!"

The inauguration of a new headman used to be attended by a great
many people. The guests, always members of the opposite moiety, were
supposed to supply the technician to make the new *pöggul*. Unfortunately, my data are not wholly unambiguous and suggest that it is
not strictly necessary for the new *pöggul* to be always presented
by relatives from the opposite moiety.

4. The significance of moiety dualism and headhunting

The ceremonies discussed in the present chapter have little in
common save that they require the cöoperation of intermarrying
groups, i.e. clan communities or settlements belonging to opposite moieties and, consequently, living at a not inconsiderable
distance from one another. Verschueren usually designates them

as connubial groups. The ceremonies described here are not the
only occasions on which these groups cooperate for purposes of a
common celebration. They also do so for marriage ceremonies, and
for the performance of final initiation ceremonies (the feast of
the *possé*) and of the various mourning rites. We are told nowhere
whether the guests participating in such celebrations belong to
clan communities or settlements from a number of different *arow*
of their moiety, or rather from one or two. In other words, we
have no information whatever regarding the effects of the marriage rules on the spatial distribution of the connubial relations of the settlement. Do the members of one settlement inter-
marry with clan communities of a wide range of other settlements
or of only one or two? A tendency towards local restriction of
the moiety exogamy is by no means improbable. It would accord
well with the fact that relations between spatially distant
groups are infrequent and sometimes hostile (Chapter I, Section 1),
as well as with the myth about Nak and Telle living on opposite
banks of the river (Chapter IV, Section 3). The mythical reference is of particular interest because it reflects a not uncommon
pattern in these parts. Wirz (1925(III):160) reports its occurrence among the Dahuk-zé on the upper Buraka. All this can hardly
be said to be anything more than an indication, however, even
though it may offer an explanation for the mysterious quadrupar-
tition in Kwél (Chapter II, page 14).

Fortunately, the description of the canoe ceremony gives us a
more substantial clue. The maker of the canoe invites the members
of his own *arow* to assist him in towing the canoe to the waterside, and later those of the most proximate *arow* of the opposite
moiety to launch the vessel. And these members of "the nearest
arow of the other moiety" include his own mother's brother! Here,
at last, is proof of a definite preference for close connubial
relations between clans belonging to adjacent or at least proximate *arow*.

But it is far more than that. The use of the term *arow*, which
is rare in Verschueren's writings, is in itself an indication
that the two intermarrying groups also cooperate in headhunting
expeditions. They must be accompanied by the *arow-yevale*. Actually, there is good reason for such cooperation. The average number
of people belonging to one *arow*, women and children included, is
a mere seventy. This implies that the number of available warriors
can hardly be more than twenty - a small striking-force indeed!
Too small, in fact, to be effectual. The canoe ceremony as such
confirms the involvement of the two *arow* in joint headhunts.
Before the actual launching the men from both *arow* go together to
the edge of the forest to call out the name of an enemy group in
order to invoke the assistance of the (*arow-*)*yevale*. Following
the launching of the canoe, the guest *arow* disappears with the
canoe for a ceremony that is performed by its *gab-elul*, who sums
up the names of all the people he has killed and then smashes a
husked coconut (often the symbol of a human head) on the stem of
the canoe. And finally, the return of the guest party resembles
too much a triumphal return from a successful head-hunt for us
not to be struck by the similarity. We might take the cooperation

of the two intermarrying *arow* for a proven fact but for Verschueren's repeated assertion that canoes are never used on headhunting expeditions (Chapter I, Section 2).

The assertion is contradicted by the details of the ceremony
reproduced above. But there are more inconsistencies in Verschueren's account. The confusion begins with Verschueren's belittle-
ment of Yéi-nan canoes, which in one place he describes as follows: "Canoes were hewn from trees without much attention to ornamentation and even without much know-how" (cf. Chapter I, Section 2). In other places he shows more appreciation, but basical-
ly he was unimpressed. This indifference to the Yéi-nan canoe
was not prompted by comparison with the canoes of other tribes,
but by the fact that he hated canoe-travel. He often said so open-
ly, and I found out why when we travelled together in Boadzi canoes
he was given to sea-sickness and could not stand the incessant
rocking caused by the standing position of the rowers. When the
Yéi told him that they never used canoes for headhunting expeditions, he was easily convinced that the vessels were unfit for
this purpose. Even so, the sea-faring coastal Marind purchased
canoes from the Yéi and we may take it for granted that they used
them on their headhunting expeditions to the lower Fly region.
The canoe of the ceremony described above definitely was a big
one. It could carry so many men that it might easily be used for
a headhunt.

Besides, it is simply inconceivable that a ceremony of such
scope and importance would have been performed for a canoe destined for individual use only. Every man had a canoe which he
used to visit his gardens or to go fishing. If such an elaborate
ceremony had to be held for every single canoe, they would have
had to attend at least four to six such celebrations a year,
either as hosts or as guests. All these inconsistencies are eliminated by the supposition that the canoe of the ceremony was really a war-canoe and that Verschueren's informants did not want to
make him any the wiser on this point. They may have felt he knew
too much as it was. In the light of Verschueren's own character-
ization of the Yéi as "inclined to craftiness and slight unreliability" (Chapter I, Section 1) this supposition is not far-fetched.

That his informants tricked him into underestimating the significance of headhunting in Yéi-nan culture is confirmed by the
emphasis that is placed on the *gab-elul*'s role as a social and
religious leader (Chapter II, pages 13f.). The ceremonial inauguration of a new *gab-elul* as well as his previous training especially in matters relating to warfare furnish convincing evidence
that, whatever else he may have been or done, the headman was
above all a war-leader. The presentation of the new headman in
the inauguration ceremony as a young man fully accords with this
function. The fact that his youth would make him less suitable
for the social functions ascribed to him confirms my doubts in
this respect.

By this stage the immense social significance of headhunting
can no longer be doubted. The seemingly innocent canoe ceremony
had to be interpreted as a feast preparatory to a headhunt per-

formed by two intermarrying *arow*. Then there are the events following on the victorious return of the party. That this was no
more than a celebration at the *arow-yevale*'s residence near the
komen is hardly credible, the less so because we are still confronted with the problem of a pig-feast possessing no other function than the strengthening of the relations between *nèkèlè-bièro*,
intermarrying groups. Are we really to attach so much weight to
the Yéi's denial at Verschueren's suggestion that it might serve
as the celebration of a successful headhunt? There is good reason
to doubt their sincerity in matters connected with headhunting.
After all, among the Marind the headhunters' feast was also a
pig-feast, and the two tribes have more in common than Verschueren cared to admit. The ceremonies introducing the pig-feast also
have a typical trait in common. Among the Marind it is the *diwazib*
who opens the feast, among the Yéi it is the *solo* and *boto* who do
so. And both tribes share the custom of presenting piglets to a
sister's husband for raising by their sister without loss of formal ownership. In all this there is nothing to prevent us from
assuming that among the Yéi-nan, too, the pig-feast formed part
of the celebration of a successful headhunt. Of course, such a
feast may have been held on other occasions as well. The avail-
ability of several sizable pigs in the community is in itself a
reason for holding one, and in this way a welcome argument for
denying every sort of relation with headhunting besides.

An even more important conclusion which must inevitably be
drawn from the analysis of the ceremonies and feasts described
here is that the notion that Yéi-nan society consists of a series
of more or less loosely connected settlements of clans of one
moiety cooperating in one common *arow* must be discarded. Instead,
it must be described as comprising a number of separate societies
made up of two or more neighbouring *arow* united by reciprocal marriage ties and cooperating in all matters of warfare and ritual,
societies which in spite of the spatial dispersion of their constituent parts can best be designated as subtribes. This is a
picture which fits in fairly well with the general pattern of
tribal organization in these parts, namely among the Boadzi, the
upper Bian Marind (and the Marind generally) and the Keraki and
other Trans-Fly peoples as far as these are hitherto sufficiently
well-known to us. As far as this resemblance goes, they are
closest, it seems, to the Trans-Fly people, among whom the delinea-
tion of the subtribes vis-à-vis each other appears to be just as
vague as among the Yéi, where even an interested observer like
Verschueren failed to recognize the institutional character of
these more comprehensive units in terms of social organization.

Chapter IX

Miscellaneous Myths

Editor's introduction

These miscellaneous myths are few in number. They are all from
Polka, with references to alternative versions from Kwél. The
stories of Section 2 are all variations on a common theme. One of
them, derived from ms. D, is in fact a combined version of vari-
ants from both Polka and Kwél. Besides, there is sound reason to
consider the story of Section 3 as just a deviant variation
on the same theme as that of Section 2. This reduces the real
number of these myths to only two. The question of whether these
myths would not have been better grouped under the heading "folk-
tales" must be left unanswered.

1. Wame, the good sister

The woman originated from Börriaw, and down to the present day it
is taboo to cut wood or pound sago there. She belonged to the Wonán-
jéi, and she was promised in marriage to a man of the Tsoggel-*jéi*
(near present-day Jejeruk). One day the Tsoggel-*jéi* invited the
Wonán-*jéi* to a feast. After going hunting together, they played
tsäddow, a game between two parties who each try to strike a bamboo
knot with a stick - not unlike hockey, but extremely dangerous. A
Wonán-*jéi* man put his foot forward, and a Tsoggel-*jéi* hit it with
his stick. A few moments later a Wonán-*jéi* wilfully hit a Tsoggel-
jéi, whereupon a real fight started. The Wonán-*jéi* lost miserably,
because the whole thing had been rigged with sinister intentions.
All the Wonán-*jéi* were killed and beheaded. But the Tsoggel-*jéi*
were not yet satisfied. They went to Börriaw to kill the people
there, too. Here in Börriaw there were also Wame and her brother
Kawat, a man who was unable to walk. Kawat was just feeding the
young dogs when Wame saw the Tsoggel people approaching. One of
them was her betrothed. She immediately took up her brother and
carried him to a pit which had been prepared for putting yams in.
They hid in the pit, which she covered with leaves and branches.
The Tsoggel people searched for her in vain - actually, she was
the cause of their entire action - and massacred all the other
people. When the Tsoggel people had gone, Wame got up and saw that
all her people were lying dead, their heads gone, carried off by
the Tsoggel.
  Wame took Kawat on her back and carried him to Kuiböiter. But
Kawat said: you have forgotten my *kupe* (club), and so she returned
to fetch her brother's club. When she returned with the *kupe*, they
decided that Kuiböiter was too dangerous. So she carried her brother
first to Jelib and then to Pörter. There they built a house. Kawat

cleared the ground, and Wame cut wood and constructed the house.

When the house was finished the dog Perabora ran off to a sago-grove, where he killed a cassowary. The dog ate part of the casso-wary, but he also swallowed sago-leaves and earth. On his return he vomited. Wame saw that there was meat in his vomit. She made a very long cord, one end of which she tied to the dog's leg, the other to Kawat's foot. The dog ran off again, and she followed the cord to the sago-groves named Walík and Terkut. She smeared her face with clay, tied the legs of the cassowary, carried the animal home and deposited it on the sleeping-platform. Kawat was pleased with his sister and said: "Well, you know how to manage things! From now on this sago-grove is yours alone". Now Wame was able to fetch sago-leaves to finish the roof of their house. They cut up the cassowary and ate it.

Kawat said: "Tomorrow try and fetch some bamboo and rattan, and also a thick piece of bamboo and reeds for arrow-shafts. Then I will teach you something." So Wame went and also brought grass for making hair-legthenings. Then Kawat made a bow and arrows for Wame. He also braided her hair and adjusted a male's hairdo of grass streamers to it. Now Wame tied her apron between her legs and put a pubic shell in front. Taking the dogs and her bow and arrows, she went to Bal, where she shot a cassowary. She decorated herself all over. On her return Kawat praised his sister again. She answered: "I found two other sago-gróves: Tambele and Kambenau". And they ate meat till they were satiated.

Then Kawat said: "Make a weir in the river". Whilst Wame con-structed the weir, Kawat made fish-traps. The fish was abundant, but Wame, carrying her catch home, forgot to remove the spikes. As she went they tore the leaves off the shrubs. Down-river a man from Walabák saw that the river had foam on its surface. He followed it up-river till he came to the fish-trap causing it. Following the trail of torn-off leaves, he discovered Wame and Kawat. Wame, on seeing the man, took her bow and arrow to shoot him down. But Kawat stopped her, saying: "Don't shoot; that man will make you a perfect husband!" And he said: "Please, enter!" Now they noted that he was a stout young man, and beautifully adorned. Kawat laid a nibung flower-spathe out for him to sit on. [A nibung flower-spathe is often used as a *wontje*, or sitting-mat.] To Wame Kawat said: "Look here, this is your prospective husband; please, be quick and pre-pare sago for him".

Toward nightfall the man wanted to return, but Kawat objected: "Why? You had better build a fire there on that side where you can sleep together". So they did, and when the next morning the man went back home, Kawat said to him: "Tell your relatives that they must take me, too, together with my sister".

One day after the man had departed Wame went out hunting again. Then the man returned, together with his kinsmen. Wame returned from the forest, beautifully adorned. She was carrying a cassowary on her back. They had a great feast. But Kawat wept, because he had seen that Wame had given her bow to her husband. They slept there one night, and together carried Kawat to Bikula.

Amost immediately after this all the Bikula people went to the Boadzi country for a headhunt. Wame went with them. Before departing, they first gave water and firewood to Kawat, who was left behind. But Kawat burnt his buttocks against the fire. Two fungi became his ears, and a nibung spathe brush lying nearby turned into a tail. Kawat changed into a pig. When Wame returned, she called from afar: "Kawat". But Kawat only answered "*Huku*", because he had turned into a pig. And Wame bewailed her brother. She threw away the human flesh she had brought with her. She refused to listen to the others, and thought: "I will fetch *gnemon*-leaves; Kawat is fond of them". So she went to the big river where she climbed a very tall *gnemon* tree. At that moment a Boadzi canoe happened to pass. It had some men aboard. They saw Wame high up in the tree. They landed and waited for her. When, unsuspectingly, she descended, a Boadzi man took her and made her his wife. Wame was never seen again, because they took her with them to the Fly River. Wame was the *yevale* of the Omboge *arow* (Telle).

> *Editor's comment*. It is almost certain that this is a mistranslation and should run "*a yevale*". "*The*" *yevale* does not make sense because in that case she would have to reside in Omboge territory. Besides, the article is a grammatical form one does not come across in these languages; at any rate it is not mentioned in Drabbe's Grammar of the Yéi language.

2. Tsakwi, the yevale of the Tawawi (Nak)

She was a very big old woman who lived at Ellepei, near the mouth of the Kolpa River (the Kolpa people are Telle). At Jejárter there lived a young man with his old mother. It was the dry season and near a well the young man had constructed a *koman* (a shooting-shelter of leaves) for hunting birds. He had made a peep-hole through which to shoot. After waiting there for quite some time, the old woman came along, laden with *ketal*, or nibung spathes used for carrying water. The boy heard the sound of the *ketal* scraping against each other and thought it was a cassowary. But then he saw that it was a woman coming to draw water. She drew one vessel after another and the boy feared that she might empty the well. In his anger he fired a blunt arrow at her buttocks. Thinking it owas a mosquito, she slapped her buttock with her hand. Then he fired again and hit her arm. All of a sudden Tsakwi realized that someone was shooting at her from the *koman*. She ran to the *koman*, etc. ...

> *Editor's comment*. In the Kwél variant the name of the woman is, alternately, *Unguru menotjer* and *Tembál*. The boy's mother is making sago somewhere nearby. The combined version of ms. D has a lengthy preamble, which is more elaborate than that of the present version. It runs as follows:

On a spit of land, at the edge of the great forest, but close to the open swamp, there lived a mother with her small son. There was no father, and the mother had to care for her boy all by herself. She went every day with her son to the sago grove near the great forest. There she made sago while the boy played nearby. One day the boy made a little bow of bamboo and arrows from sagoleaf-ribs all by himself. He shot a butterfly and brought it to his mother, asking if he could eat it. The mother was scraping sago-pith from the stem. She smiled and said: "No, that's impossible". He then shot a small lizard and showed it his mother while she was kneading the pulp. Having little time to lose she just smiled and said no. Again the boy went out shooting. Now he shot an iguana, and his mother taught him how to prepare the iguana. That night they ate of the iguana together, and the boy was happy. From that time onward the boy provided his mother with meat for both of them. He shot pigeons and bush-hens, and his mother made sago.

Once, during the dry season, there was no water anywhere except in a well at the edge of the forest. By now the boy had grown up. He had a strong bamboo bow. Near the well he constructed a *koman* from where he watched for birds coming to the well to drink. Sudden- ly, a big woman came from the forest. "*Uguru, uguru*", she cried, and cursed at the mosquitoes which stung her. When she arrived at the well, she abused all the animals of the forest because they had soiled her well. The boy was frightened. When she had gone he ran to his mother to tell her what he had seen. But the mother thought that it must have been a cassowary and told him to shoot it. He went back to the *koman* and waited for her return. Again she came from the forest. His first arrow grazed her elbow. She thought a mosquito had stung her, ...

Editor's comment. Here we return to the main variant, which re- lates the remainder of the story in a more concise form. The Kwél variant of ms. B differs mainly in that the woman here is called Tembál or Wienggum.

She ran to the *koman*, put her long arms around it and crushed the whole thing. But the boy ducked out and ran off to his mother in Jerárter. He explained everything to her. She concealed him in a big nibung spathe, which she suspended from the ridge-pole of the house.

Following the scent of the boy[1], Tsakwi arrived at the house. She was in a rage, but the boy's mother did not tell her anything. Tsakwi finally saw the nibung spathe hanging there. "What is in that?", she asked. "My kava cuttings", said the mother. But Tsakwi had already opened the bundle. "Ha", she said, "that is good. Come here. From now on you are my husband." And she took the boy as her husband. They stayed there for two nights, but neither the boy nor his mother were happy. The mother went into the forest to find her- self a black ant-nest. She took it with her and carved it into human shape. Then she smoothened the contraption with candlenut oil and concealed it in the tall grass near her hut.

Toward nightfall Tsakwi returned with the boy. The mother secret- ly informed her son of her plans. About midnight she awakened her son, and together they put the carved ant-nest in the boy's place. Then they fled. Near the Widj they chanced upon two men, Marmarde- geraw and Belludegeraw. They said to them: "A big woman is running after us. If you come across her, please take her and marry her if you like, but hold her." Tsakwi, angered by the deceit, was already

following them. But the two men took her to wife. The mother and
her son had meanwhile proceeded to the upper course of the river
and arrived in the territory of Bogodes (Kwél).

Editor's comment. The alternative versions of the myth contain a
number of additional details which are of some interest. They
note that the boy had to work hard for his wife, who compelled
him to fetch firewood and to delouse her constantly, which latter
is another reference to her animal-like nature. In this context
another detail is of interest. On their flight the mother and son
have attached *maker* (cf. Chapter VII, page 81f.) to the shrubs
to trick her into taking the wrong way. But Tsakwi - or whatever
else she may be called - does not heed the *maker*; she just follows
the scent.
    In these variant versions, the two men who must marry Tsakwi are
crocodiles, the one a white, the other a black one. In one, these
crocodiles ware made by the mother. When the old woman, encouraged
by the mother's assertion that the water is not deep, tries to
cross the river, the two crocodiles, trying to take her as their
wife, each take one half of the ogress, the white one the upper
half, the black one the lower half.
    The mother is an interesting character. Trying to cross the
river, she asks various trees in succession to bend their trunks
to let her and her son pass over them. But the wild fig-tree
apologizes because its legs are crooked, and another tree because
its belly is too fat. Only the long and straight nibung palm com-
plies. They walk across the river over its bent stem, whereupon,
at the mother's invitation, the nibung palm straightens itself
again and resumes its original shape. In all this the mother is
a good, ancestress-like character. She is even so not called a
yevale, a term which in Verschueren's commentary on the story is
reserved for Tsakwi, whose character resembles far more that of
an ogress, an animal-like kind of creature, than that of an ancestress. This non-human character is emphasized by yet another detail in the two alternative readings. In both, the mother has
equipped the ant-nest imitationoof her son with two horns on the
head, a feature by which the spirits of the dead are designated
(Chapter VII, p. 81 and note 4). The ogre-like nature of the big
woman recurs in the third and final myth of this chapter.

3. *Tanggole, the old woman (yevale of Tawawi)*

Introductory note. There are two versions of this myth. The first
is found in ms. B under the heading used by me here. It is incomplete, breaking off in the middle of the story. Verschueren notes
that probably Tanggole should be identified with Tsakwi, i.e.
with Tembál. The full text is found in ms. D under the heading
"The Bad Old Woman". The author adds here that this story derives
from Kwél, Polka and Bupul (in that order) but is located on the
Obat River. He further states that the present version ignores
local differences. The story, according to Verschueren, forms
part of the same cycle as the one related under number 2 (by me)
and may be regarded as a sequel to it. He says: "If considered

as a sequel to that story, its narration may be begun as follows":2

At another time, Unguru, the Bad Woman, was living in a settlement
on the Obat River. In this settlement there lived a great many
children. One day Unguru said to the children: "You all come along
with me; we are going to play". The children liked this, and followed the old woman skipping and dancing. When they arrived at the
bank of the river, the old woman said: "Boys, you must put a weir
in the river and make fish-traps to catch fish. And you, girls,
must plait baskets, put some ants into them, and place them on the
bed of the river to catch shrimps". They all did as the old woman
said, because they did not know that she wanted to keep all the
fish and shrimps for herself.

After some time a large quantity of fish and shrimps had been collected, and the old woman said: "It is allright now; you had better
sit down in the shade with me and I will teach you a new game". The
old woman deliberately seated herself under a wild fig-tree which
was full of fruit. Here she taught them the game of piling hands.
The first child puts one hand on the hand of the next, who covers
it with his second hand; the first then does the same, after which
a third and a fourth join in, and so on till the hands of all the
children form a high pile. Then they move their hands rhythmically
up and down while singing a song like the following:

5 3 3 5   3 3   3 5   3 3 3 3 . 5   5 5   5   7 . 5 0
Takare re-po re-po sam-po-re po-re ko-re dam-da leh   ah

But the children, seeing the wild figs, abandoned their game and
climbed the tree. The old woman acted as though she were angry and
ordered them to come down. But the children were hungry, because the
old woman had taken all their fish and shrimps, and they went on
gathering fruits. Then the old woman said: "Tree, grow and become
very tall!" And the tree grew so high that the children did not
dare to descend. They called: "Grandmother, what shall we do?"
Unguru answered" "Just leap down". Immediately, one of the boys
leapt down because the old woman stood ready to catch him. But she
let him fall to the ground, took a stick and beat him to death. The
other children got terribly frightened, and called out: "Grandmother,
why did you not catch him?" "He was too quick", she replied, "I was
not yet ready. But now you may safely leap down." But the others
who leapt down suffered the same fate; they all fell to the ground,
where the old woman killed them with a piece of wood. A few of the
children were so frightened that they turned into birds and flew
off.

The old woman collected all the fish and shrimps. She also cut
off the fingers of the children and wrapped them up in a separate
package. She hid the corpses of the children in a bush-hen's nest,
and then returned to the village. There the people asked her:
"Where are our children?" But the old one answered: "They are a
handful! Try as I did to bring them home, they went on playing in
the bush!" And she made a fire and began roasting her fish. But
the people were afraid, and the men rose to go in search. At that
particular moment one of the dogs ran off with the package with

the children's fingers which the old woman had just placed on the
fire. She cried out: "Quick, the dog has stolen my shrimps". A young
man took the package off the dog and saw that it was not filled with
shrimps but with children's fingers. He warned the villagers. Because they knew that the old hag was a witch they devised a ruse.
They prepared for a headhunt and told the old woman: "Grandmother,
we are going on a headhunt. We will first build you a good strong
house and provide it with food and water, so that nothing may happen to you whilst we are away". They did accordingly, using only
perfectly dry wood. And the water vessels which the women hung
against its walls were empty. The sago bags were empty, too. Finally, they invited the old woman to enter the house, and then barri-
caded the entrance. The old woman smiled; she thought: "How helpful
they all are". Having said good-bye, they all departed, but that
very night the men returned and set the house afire. The old woman
could not get out, and she was burnt together with the house and
everything in it.

Editor's comment. The walled house is an a-typical feature. It
suggests that the story (or this specific version of it) may be
of foreign origin. In other respects, however, it does not differ
markedly from those of Section 2. The unfinished version of ms.
B even has the motif of the old woman's wish to be deloused in
common with them. All the old women of both sections can be characterized as typical ogresses, supernatural, infra-human beings:
they eat their own people, suffer from an abundance of lice, and
find their way by scent. As such, they cannot be equated with
ancestors in any way. Even so, they are designated by the term
yevale.
   A point of particular interest is the non-occurrence of male
ogres. These infra-human beings are all females. In point of
fact, death and evil are closely associated with the female sex.
The really dangerous illness is the female illness inflicted by
Baderam. The dead are buried in the *wake*. And the deadly part of
the club, the *kupe*, is a symbolic representation of the female
genitals and is closely associated with the great mother of the
Boadzi, the Atu. She accompanied her son Ndiwe on his journey to
Yéi-nan territory, on which journey he provided their ancestors
with a *kupe*, which later became the *komen* where, in time, an
arow-yevale took up his residence. It is always a female who in-
stigates a headhunting raid: among the Marind Sobra, among the
Boadzi Atu. And the focal figure of the Marind Imo ritual, the
tribal ancestress, is referred to as Bad Woman or Excrement Woman.
Among the goddesses, Atu has one specific detail in common with
the ogress Tanggole, i.e. her association with the nest of a
bush-hen (Van Baal 1966:595). Unfortunately our information is
very incomplete. A large part of Yéi-nan mythology has remained
concealed from us, and all sorts of questions remain unanswered,
such as, for instance, the lexicographical question of whether
komen and *koman* are totally different words or not. All the same,
there can be no doubt about the Yéi's association of the female
sex with death and evil.

Chapter X

Editor's Epilogue

The analysis of Verschueren's data has provided a fascinating picture of the life and culture of a southern lowland tribe, composed of a number of fairly vaguely delimitated segmented societies, and characterized by moiety dualism, separation and antagonism between the sexes, and an immense urge for male assertion. The Yéi-nan are unique in several respects. First of all in the way they give spatial form to the separation of the sexes. This compensates for the inferior position of the women by creating an exceptional opportunity for collective protection of the individual females. In the second place they are unique in making their initiation ritual dependent upon an event in the women's community, the first menstruation of a girl. Thirdly because of the uncommon emphasis on the maleness of the men through their total identification with the phallic symbol. In the fourth place in the demonstration of the male power of fertility by asserting that males, too, have the ability to bleed. And finally, in the unusually elaborate manner of exhibiting the spoils of their headhunts in a spot on the boundary separating the sexes in the communal house as though to express the idea that both sexes have a part in the matter: the women (who care for the dead) on the side of death, the men on that of life and fertility. After all, the women accompany the men on their headhunting raids and participate in the cannibalistic meal following it (cf. the myth of Wame).

It is not these facts in themselves which determine the difference between the Yéi and the tribes surrounding them. It is rather the degree of emphasis. A spatial separation of men and women is common to all of them, but the Yéi are the only ones to give it this unusual form. Initiation, too, is common to all these tribes, but no other of these combines it with a first menstruation. The identification of the males with a phallic symbol is not unusual, either, but again no other tribe expresses this as emphatically as the Yéi do in the köllu-köllu rites. Finally, the display of the heads captured on a war raid is common practice everywhere, but the place for this is always the men's house, and the heads are never exhibited in combination with the remains of a cannibal repast as is done in the morbid still-life adorning the central post of the Yéi-nan communal house.

The inordinate claims of male potency and emphasis on the males' contribution to fertility generally in the köllu-köllu ritual, the sexual symbolism inherent in the headhunting ritual, and the great significance given to this symbolism in Yéi-nan culture as a whole all concur to confirm the theory that, fundamentally, the males suffer from strong feelings of inferiority vis-à-vis their females and feel they must compensate this inferiority by acts of violence. It is this theory which I hesitantly put forward in my book *Dema*, in a general theoretical context in *Man's Quest for Partnership* (1981), and with specific reference to the Marind-anim in my contribution to G.H. Herdt's book on ritualized homosexuality in Melanesia (in the press). The Yéi-nan data (which were perfectly new to me) have now strengthened me in this supposition, even to the extent that I now feel I should have given McKinley's view that headhunting is primarily a religious rite more thought in my book of 1981. But this is not the point here.

The point is that Verschueren's data are thoroughly convincing. He did not realize their purport and tried to use them as proof of the moral superiority of the Yéi over the Marind - a vain attempt, but for this very reason an indubitable confirmation both of their worth and of the author's sincerity. We are much indebted to Verschueren for his observations. They have opened up a surprising new view of a quite extraordinary way of life and thinking, enriching our knowledge of the diversity of human life and worldviews with a new and valuable model.

As a conscientious, sincere missionary Verschueren despised many of his parishioners' customs and beliefs. He loved the people in spite of this and tried to understand what motivated their to him scandalous views and behaviour. Verschueren was not an anthropologist, but his love of mankind and his interest in his fellow-men turned him into one of those wonderful ethnographers who are the real masters of our discipline in that they provide us with ever new models of human behaviour and expression.

Notes

Chapter I

1 The Indonesian name for a variety of fruit trees of the *Eugenia* genus.
2 Verschueren writes "sorcery", but what he means is "magic".
3 This, in my opinion unfair, generalization ignores the typically Marind character of such songs as *samb-zi*, *weiko-zi* and *yarut*. What Verschueren had in mind was apparently the *gad-zi*, as the kind of song more commonly heard in later times.

Chapter II

1 In this context Verschueren uses the words "settlement" and "group" interchangeably, but not the word "clan". This is significant. He must have had an intuitive idea of the ambiguity of the term. By avoiding the word "clan", his description following immediately below fully corroborates the supposition that it is the house-community which is the holder of territorial rights.
2 One should not over-emphasize the effect of this concentration. At the time it took place the Yéi-nan counted fewer than 2,000 people, the equivalent of the population of at most 27 viable settlements. Besides, bigger settlements were already in existence. A reduction of this number to 9, though upsetting the system, is relatively moderate.
3 There is one possible exception. Buwĭm (Bupul) has a *jéi* called Wan, Tsarup (Kwél) one by name of Wán. There is only the difference of the *a* and *á*. Being unfamiliar with the language, I am unable to decide whether the difference is significant or not.

Chapter III

1 That elopement of a widow cannot have been such a rare event as is suggested here will be argued in Chapter VII, Section 4.
2 I presume that this expresses the opinion of the missionary rather than that of the people concerned.
3 For evidence that older women had their doubts on this point, see p. 33.
4 For an explanation of this enigmatic statement the reader is referred to Chapter VI. Unfortunately, a full explanation cannot be given because the myth to which Verschueren is referring could not be found in his papers. In its absence, the supposition that Baderam causes pregnancy seems far-fetched and unwarranted.

Chapter IV

1 Verschueren is not consistent in the use of the terms upper and middle, except that he always locates the Boadzi on the upper

Fly. In fact, this should be the middle Fly. Apparently, the place meant in the present case is somewhere near the southern border of the Boadzi territory.

2 The translation is mine, and is given with the reservation that I do not know the word *gön*. But *bu* = you, while Dambu and Kello are names of *jéi*, the one Telle, the other Nak (cf. inter alia the list at the end of Chapter II under Tanas: Udöp and Boad).

3 Apart from the fact that it refers to something else, the quotation is also slipshod. Verschueren often felt irritated by Wirz's expositions, which he tended too easily to regard as being insufficiently well founded.

4 This looks like a personal name. But cf. Chapter VII, Section 1, where the boy who calls for a canoe uses the word *kwor* and not the term *kogwie*, which according to Geurtjens' *Woordenboek* is the word for canoe (pp. 416-7).

5 The argument is too far-fetched to require specific refutation. Apparently it was inspired by the author's wish to underline the fact that they should not be considered as ancestors, the point on which he disagrees with Wirz.

Chapter V

1 In this part of the manuscript the author no longer speaks of *korár bö* (as in Chapter II, Section 2), but of *korár ben* or *kudyir ben*. *Ben* means "fire" (Geurtjens *Woordenboek* p. 420-1), and it is the fire, kindled by the boys, which is the key subject in this passage. The passage ends with the remark that *korár* or *kudyir* must in this context be interpreted as "open place" and not in its literal meaning of "enclosure" or "fence".

2 This pious assertion sounds too good to be true.

3 The author does not explain what this implies, nor what happened to an "unsuccessful" candidate.

4 We must assume that every boy went on this pathetic errand alone and in strict secrecy.

5 Note that Udöp and Bomön are Telle *jéi* of Bupul and Tanas. This justifies the conclusion that, in spite of what has been said on this point in Chapter I (see page 5) the *yevale* cult is definitely practised in the northern settlements.

6 The exact meaning of this statement is not clear, but anyway it suggests some kind of clan or totem relation (cf. also pp. 71 and 72).

7 Note the explicit identification of the *kupör* and Orei.

Chapter VI

1 Ms. A stresses that an incomplete confession necessarily leads to failure of the treatment and that for this reason the patient's friends help him refresh his memory concerning the faults he may have committed. This is not necessarily in contradiction with the statement that inefficacy of the treatment is due to the healer's failure to extract the whole of the apron. This need not be more than the means by which the consequences of incomplete confession announce themselves.

Chapter VII

1   A hardwood tree with a very long life.
2   *Kwor* = canoe.
3   On the identity of the *tang* with the *anda*-fish, and via the
    latter its association with penis, snake and bullroarer in
    Marind-anim lore, see Van Baal 1966:270f., 486f.
4   The masks representing the spirits of the dead among the Marind
    are also horned. Probably these horns represent the headgear of
    bird of paradise feathers worn by the living. Cf. Van Baal 1966:
    619 and 779.

Chapter IX

1   The motif of her following of the scent recurs in all three
    variants. Apparently, it is meant to indicate her animal nature.
2   This implies that the old woman is given different names, and
    that the name Unguru, borrowed from the composite version of
    Ms. D, need not be a name that is often used at all.

Bibliography

Baal, J. van
1963   'The Cult of the Bull-Roarer in Australia and Southern
          New Guinea', *Bijdragen tot de Taal-, Land- en Volkenkunde*
          119(2):201-14.
1966   *Dema. Description and Analysis of Marind-anim Culture
          (South New Guinea)*, with the collaboration of Father J.
          Verschueren msc, Translation Series KITLV 9, The Hague:
          Nijhoff.
1971   'In Memoriam Pater Jan Verschueren, m.s.c.', *Bijdragen tot
          de Taal-, Land- en Volkenkunde* 127(4):490-1.
1981   *Man's Quest for Partnership*, Assen: Van Gorcum.
[In the   'The Dialectics of Sex in Marind Anim Culture', in: G.H.
press]   Herdt (ed.), *Ritualized Homosexuality in Melanesia*.

Boelaars, J.H.M.C.
1950   *The Linguistic Position of South-Western New Guinea*, Lei-
          den: Brill.

Boldingh, L.G.
1951/52   'Bevolkingscijfers van Zuid-Nieuw-Guinea', *Indonesië* 5:
          41-72, 167-85.

Drabbe, P.
1954   *Talen en Dialecten van Zuid-West Nieuw-Guinea*, Micro Biblio-
          theca Anthropos, vol. 11, Posieux (Fribourg). (Microfilm.)

Geurtjens, H.
1933   *Marindineesch-Nederlandsch Woordenboek*, Verhandelingen van
          het Koninklijk Bataviaasch Genootschap van Kunsten en We-
          tenschappen 71-5 (including a comparative wordlist of the
          languages of adjacent tribes). (Abbreviated as *Woordenboek*.)

Landtman, G.
1917   *The Folk-tales of the Kiwai Papuans*, Acta Societatis
          Scientiarum Fennicae 47, Helsingfors.
1927   *The Kiwai Papuans of British New Guinea*, London: MacMillan.

McKinley, Robert
1976   'Human and Proud of it! A Structural Treatment of Head-
          hunting Rites and the Social Definition of Enemies', in:
          G.N. Appell (ed.), *Studies in Borneo Societies*: *Social
          Process and Anthropological Explanation*, Northern Illinois
          University, Center for Southeast Asian Studies, report 12.

Nevermann, Hans
1942   'Die Je-nan', *Baessler-Archiv* 24:87-221.

Rapport
1958   *Rapport van het bevolkingsonderzoek onder de Marind-anim*
          van Nederlands Zuid Nieuw-Guinea, South Pacific Commission,
          Population Studies - S 18 Project (mimeographed), by Dr.
          S. Kooijman, Father J. Verschueren m.s.c., M. Dorren and
          L. Veeger, with appendices by Dr. Norma MacArthur and Dr.
          L. Luyken. (Abbreviated as *Report Depopulation Team.*)

Verschueren, J.
1947/48   'Het mensenoffer op de zuidkust van Nederlands Nieuw
          Guinea', *Indonesië* I:437-70.

Verslag
1920   *Verslag van de Militaire Exploratie van Nederlandsch-Nieuw-*
          Guinee 1907-1915, Weltevreden: Landsdrukkerij.

Williams, F.E.
1936   *Papuans of the Trans-Fly*, Oxford: Clarendon Press.

Wirz, Paul
1925   *Die Marind-anim von Holländisch-Süd-Neu-Guinea*, Teil III,
          Hamburgische Universität, Abhandlungen aus dem Gebiet der
          Auslandskunde, Reihe B, Band 16, Hamburg: Friederichsen.

Woordenboek
          See H. Geurtjens.

PLATE I. Drawings by the mission teacher Renwarin.

Fig. 1. Items of mourning-dress (cf. p. 77). Heavy mourning involves a, b, c, d, e, f. Medium mourning involves b, c, d, e. Light mourning involves only kamartje, which is only worn by young people and which is less wide.

SOYA FOR WOMEN

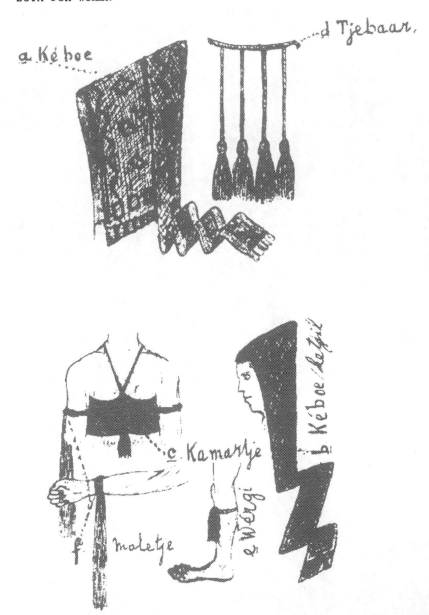

Fig. 2. Objects suspended near infant's cradle (cf. p. 34).

Fig. 3. Soté; young palm-leaf shoots (cf. p. 67).

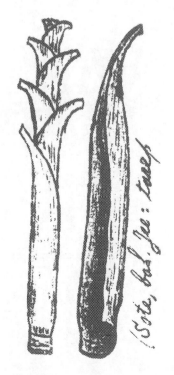

Printed in the United States
By Bookmasters